THE

FREE GRANT LANDS

OF

CANADA.

Yours very Sincerely
Thomas Mc Murray

THE

FREE GRANT LANDS

OF

CANADA,

FROM PRACTICAL EXPERIENCE OF BUSH FARMING IN THE
FREE GRANT DISTRICTS OF

MUSKOKA AND PARRY SOUND,

BY

THOS. McMURRAY, J. P.,

ONE OF THE FIRST SETTLERS IN DRAPER, AND EX-REEVE OF THE UNITED
TOWNSHIPS OF DRAPER, MACAULAY STEPHENSON, ETC., ETC.

BRACEBRIDGE, ONT., CANADA:

PRINTED AND PUBLISHED AT THE OFFICE OF THE "NORTHERN ADVOCATE."
1871.

This edition published 2002 by Fox Meadow Creations and Brad Hammond
Foreword © 2002 by Brad Hammond

Trade distribution
Fox Meadow Creations
Box 5401, Huntsville, Ontario P1H 2K7
www.foxmeadowbooks.com

NATIONAL LIBRARY OF CANADA CATALOGUING IN PUBLICATION DATA

McMurray, Thomas, b. 1831
The free grant lands of Canada : from practical experience of bush farming in the
free grant districts of Muskoka and Parry Sound / Thomas McMurray.

Reprint. First published: Bracebridge, Ont. : Northern Advocate, 1871.
ISBN 0-9681452-6-4

1. Muskoka (Ont. : District) – Description and travel. 2. Parry Sound (Ont. :
District) – Description and travel. 3. Muskoka (Ont. : District) – Economic
conditions. 4. Parry Sound (Ont. : District) – Economic conditions.
5. Land settlement – Ontario – Muskoka (District).
6. Land settlement – Ontario – Parry Sound (District). I. Title.

HD319.O5M3 2002   971.3'1603   C2002-902247-9

Front cover design by Lorrie Szekat / Typesetting by Fox Meadow Creations
Set in Tyrnavia
Printed in Canada on acid-free paper by Métrolitho

*This edition is not a facsimile reprint of the original book. The text, however, has been
replicated unabridged with no editing. The interior design follows the general scheme of
McMurray's production, with concessions to different printing and binding methods and
a somewhat larger type size. Running heads have been adjusted to suit the revised format.
Illustrations in the original book are retained except for a fold-out map of southern
Ontario, of which only the portion relevant to McMurray's account has been reproduced.*

TITLE PAGE SPREAD
From the 1871 edition, the original title page and portrait of Thomas McMurray

FRONT COVER PHOTOGRAPH
Early farmers in Muskoka District (courtesy of Barbara Paterson)

FOREWORD

TO THE 2002 EDITION

by Brad Hammond

————————

THOMAS MCMURRAY was both a chronicler of his times and a dreamer. He was a moralist, a temperance man, and a firm believer in God and the Empire. Born in Paisley, Scotland, in 1831, McMurray had been to sea and adventured to America before settling temporarily in Belfast, Ireland, where he started a family and became connected to the Irish Temperance League. By 1861, the year McMurray emigrated to Canada at age 30, the great cities of Britain were burdened by disease and overcrowding. Charles Dickens was alive and well and about to gain ascendancy as the writer of his era. Ireland was in the throes of famine and the Empire was bogged down in the farthest corners of the earth. It was the height of the Victorian era, and McMurray was very much a man of his times.

One thing that Thomas McMurray never pretended to be was an historian, although his writings are widely quoted as historical reference. After more than one hundred and thirty years, it is too easy to lose sight of the fact that his book, *The Free Grant Lands of Canada*, was intended for a contemporary audience. Sandwiched between sound advice to emigrants and McMurray's vivid descriptions of Muskoka in its earliest days of settlement, are the hopes and ambitions of an entrepreneur and businessman. Transplanted to the romantic hinterland of the new Free Grant district, it probably didn't take long for McMurray to realize life would be easier if there were a town within two day's travel, a school for his children, and a market for his talents. As one of the earliest settlers, McMurray soon became a principal in promoting and advancing settlement in Muskoka.

He quickly immersed himself in local politics as first reeve of the United Townships of Draper, Macaulay, Stephenson and Ryde, began the first newspaper, the *Northern Advocate*, which printed its premiere edition in Parry Sound in 1869 before moving to Bracebridge, and involved himself in attracting settlers, business, and even a railway. He was a "mover and shaker" with the belief that God, respect for the Sabbath, and a willingness to work were the three most important requirements for success. It wouldn't hurt, of course, if you bought his book, advertised in his newspaper, and diligently followed his advice.

There were times, however, when even that wasn't enough. In 1871, while writing *The Free Grant Lands of Canada*, McMurray could not foresee the effects of a financial crash in the neighbouring United States, nor could he imagine that within two years his businesses would fail. His impressive new brick building in Bracebridge, known as the McMurray Block, with its apartments, stores, and McMurray's own office with vaulted ceiling and enormous window, was soon torn down. The *Northern Advocate* was sold and in 1873 McMurray was in Toronto, where he published his *Temperance Lectures, with Autobiography*. By 1874 he reappears in Parry Sound as Crown Lands Agent and founding publisher of the *North Star* newspaper. Following the sale of that enterprise in March 1879, he reinvented himself as a full-time advocate and lecturer on behalf of temperance, his lifelong passion.

There is little in local archives to shed light upon the later life of Thomas McMurray. We know that his impact upon the political and economic life of both Muskoka and Parry Sound was vast and that he was deeply devoted to the growth of his community. We know when he arrived and when he left, but we don't know much about what became of him following the marriage of his third daughter Fanny Hazelton in June 1879, as reported in the *North Star*. Indeed, his next appearance in local print is the August 23, 1900, *North Star* article headlined "Thomas McMurray Dead," which suggests he no longer resided in either Parry Sound or Muskoka.

According to Robert J. Boyer's wonderful reference book, *A Good Town Grew Here*, Thomas McMurray's son Gilman passed through Bracebridge shortly afterward, returning from the Boer War, en route to his boyhood home at Parry Sound. The trail ends there for local historians.

The Free Grant Lands of Canada has become a rare and much sought after book since its original printing in 1871. It is with pleasure, then, that we now make it available for readers to enjoy McMurray's advice from the comfort of the twenty-first century. His vision and determination were formidable, as were the hardships we are sure he faced as an early pioneer of the district. It was his ambition and entrepreneurial spirit, foreseeing and advocating tens of thousands of farms and homes, which helped carve Muskoka and Parry Sound from the wilderness. It was the failure to fulfill his dream, however, which may have provided the greatest legacy to our district.

This new edition of *The Free Grant Lands of Canada*, the first book ever published in Muskoka, would not have been possible without the assistance of the following people:

Gary Long for his immediate enthusiasm, research, and continuous efforts to correct any "Bradley-isms" which crept into the transcription;

Lorrie Szekat for her artistic contributions;

My friends and associates at *Muskoka Times* and *Vintage Muskoka*;

Jim Cumberland for adding a rare first edition copy to my collection;

The girls who lured me into Betty Rintoul's high school typing class, teaching me that "hunt and peck" was not an adequate motto in life;

Louise, for her support and patience during my frequent absences and more frequent bouts of absent-mindedness, and for joining five generations of Hammonds in Muskoka in teaching me the true meaning of "home."

Thanks especially to my parents, Orv and Fran Hammond, who taught me the value of the open road, an open door, an open book, and an open mind. A tough act to follow.

I take full credit for any and all typographical errors or mistakes not found in the original text of *The Free Grant Lands of Canada*.

Brad Hammond
District of Muskoka
July, 2002

Dedication.

———

To the Ontario Government, in consideration of what it has done to improve the navigation and promote the development of the Free Grant Districts, this work is respectfully dedicated by

THE AUTHOR.

A Card of Thanks.

———————

The Author hereby expresses his obligations to those persons who supplied much of the information contained in this work, and takes this opportunity of returning his sincere thanks for the prompt attention which was paid to his enquiries.

PREFACE.

The fact of my being the first settler in the Township of Draper and first Reeve of the united Townships of Draper, Macaulay, Stephenson, &c., in the District of Muskoka, has given me considerable notoriety, hence I have received letters from all parts of the world asking for information about the country, and, although hard pressed for time I have always willingly responded to those appeals; but, in the opinion of the Author, the time has now arrived in the history of the settlement, when something more is wanted than a courteous reply to letters of enquiry. There are tens of thousands in the United Kingdom, and many even in Canada who are anxious to know whether this country is fit for settlement or not.

With a view, therefore, to put them in possession of the most reliable information, this work has been written. Having resided in the settlement now for about ten years, during which I have closely watched its growth and development, and being in possession of many facts which must prove both interesting and instructive, I desire to give them the fullest publicity, so that others may be benefited by my knowledge and experience.

THOMAS McMURRAY.

Bracebridge,
21st February, 1871.

CONTENTS.

HISTORY

OF THE

EARLY SETTLEMENT OF MUSKOKA.

The Road was commenced at Washago, in 1858; Messrs. St. George and O'Brien were the contractors.

In the fall of 1859, Mr. R.J. Oliver was appointed Locating Agent at $4 per diem, under the Government of the Hon. John A. Macdonald; Mr. P.M. Vankoughnet being Crown Lands' Commissioner. On the 1st of October, 1859, he met the settlers at the Severn Bridge and issued about 17 locations—(on the Road only)—James H. Jackson, William Johnson, and John Young, James McCabe, David Leith, and the Simingtons, were the first settlers in the Townships of Morrison and Muskoka. A small shanty had been opened as a tavern, and was kept by a brother-in-law (Mr. Swift) of the late John Tipping, Esq., J.P., of Orillia, who purchased 5 acres off lot No. 1, west from William Johnston. Donald Ferguson, a brave Highland Scotchman, was the first settler in the Township of Draper. At this period the road only extended to the South Falls, and the bridge was not built; but "Donald," nothing daunted, crossed the river and located on a lovely spot close to the Falls on the north side of the river. While lots on the road were located in the fall of 1859, it was not till 1861 that the lands in the Townships of Morrison, Muskoka, Draper and Macaulay, were thrown upon the market, and at the same time Mr. R.J. Oliver was appointed Crown Lands' Agent. It was in the month of May, in this same year, that the writer became a resident of Draper—before the

Township was entirely surveyed. I cannot but refer here to the bitter opposition which was manifested towards the Government by a portion of the Press and a number of gentlemen, for attempting to open up this part of Ontario; every form of misrepresentation and abuse was sought after and circulated, and it was even asserted that it was only to "afford situations for their friends" that the country was opened up. The town of Barrie figured very conspicuously in their opposition to the settling up on the North; among the fault finders we might name B., L. and M.; but as a sample of the opinion in which Muskoka was held in those days, we may just state that M. told our author that "he would not pay the taxes on a single 100 acres of land for all the land north of the Severn." Muskoka has been much abused, still it had a few earnest friends who have done their duty nobly. Mr. R.J. Oliver fought many a hard battle and silenced many a foe. We find, on examination, that he wrote not less than 83 Editorials and Letters in defence of the country. Mr. J.C. McMullen has also been a true friend of the District; and, by his willing pen, has won many friends in the settlement.

Prominent amongst the early settlers stand the names of Mr. and Mrs. McCabe; they opened a tavern at Gravenhurst in 1861, and many a worn-out traveller has been glad to see their unpretentious log cabin where they might rest their weary limbs and get some refreshment to sustain nature. Never shall the writer forget his first interview with "Mother McCabe." When he arrived there, he was hungry and footsore; but he met with an "Irish welcome," and a dinner was served up by "Mother McCabe" which would not have disgraced any Hotel north of Toronto. The old log shanty looked dull outside, but within all was cleanliness and order; her clean white curtains kept out the musquitoes in summer and cold in winter, while her feather beds afforded sweet rest to many a weary land-seeker. How welcome was the sight of the dim low light through the bush, to the weary traveller, can only be fully appreciated by the early pedestrians when no horses or vehicles were on the road; there are hundreds in the settlement who remember them, and some of them have cause to bless "Mother McCabe" for her generosity. The first death in the settlement was that of poor Johnston; he was drowned at the Severn bridge one Sunday whilst fishing. The poor widow struggled hard with her two little boys—the elder not more than 9 years—and, with their help, she managed before she died to clear about 8 or 9 acres; but, alas, fell in the harness.

Mrs. William Gardiner and Mrs. Thomas McMurray gave birth to the first children in Draper, and Mrs. John Kelly to the first in Monck.

The first lumber mill in the settlement was built in 1861, by John Everbeck, a German, on the Kah-she-she-bog-a-mog River, near Sparrow Lake, in the Township of Morrison; the second was erected by James Grant; the first grist mill also by James Grant, on the same stream where it crosses the Muskoka Road, 5 miles north of Washago.

THE

FREE GRANT LANDS

OF

MUSKOKA.

SITUATION.

Muskoka is conveniently situated, being only 121 miles distant from the City of Toronto. Its location is in direct line in the overland route to the great North-West. Parties leaving Toronto in the morning can reach the settlement during the summer months in a day, and the trip is one of the most pleasant and attractive possible. The eastern and western boundaries are situated within and between 79° and 80° west from Greenwich. The geographical position of the settlement is good, forming as it does almost a bee-line of travel from Liverpool to Vancouver. It is the shortest route by hundreds of miles from the Atlantic to the Pacific. Who can predict the future of this section of Ontario? If our Canadian Government would but manifest that enterprise which the importance of the case demands, before five years this route would be open.

EXTENT.

The District of Muskoka comprises say 40 townships, of about 40,000 acres each, covering an area of over one million five hundred thousand acres of land, capable of affording homes for one hundred thousand souls.

CLIMATE.

The climate is mild, taking into consideration the latitude 45°, N. —. There is here perfect summer and perfect winter. The

4

bracing atmosphere is very conducive to health, rendering it one of the healthiest climates under the sun. Save in cases of accident the doctor is seldom seen here. There are slight falls of snow in November, but it never lies till the beginning of December, when winter sets in. Snow continues to fall at intervals, till, in February, it sometimes attains a depth of 3 or 4 feet. In March it begins to settle, but is not finally gone till the 8th or 10th of April. In summer there is more moisture here than further south, owing to the greater elevation and vicinity to the lakes, from which cool breezes prevail. There is freedom from drought which is so mischievous below, rendering the district peculiarly favorable for stock-raising and the dairy. Owing to the salubrity of the climate and the mineral nature of the water, many who were sickly before coming here, have since become healthy and strong. If we have somewhat more snow, we can fairly claim that, almost as soon as the snow is gone, the land is dry for the plough, and soon ready for the seed. Wheat sown in the last week of April will be ripe by the second week of August.

Rains are abundant in spring and autumn. Fogs are rare. The hottest months of summer are July and August, and the coldest months of winter are January and February. During the winter months we enjoy almost without interruption a fine clear sky, and the atmosphere is peculiarly bracing. The Indian summer, which generally occurs in October, is a delightful time of the year. The sleighing season, in winter, is also a pleasant period.

THE SOIL.

While large flats of clay are found in many places, the soil is mostly of a loamy nature. The average amount fit for cultivation will probably be two-thirds. One gratifying fact is that the land, on being cleared and cultivated, has turned out much better than was anticipated.

TIMBER.

The timber south of Muskoka Falls is principally composed of pine of fair quality; north of the Falls, a very perceptible change is noticeable, the great proportion being composed of hardwood, consisting of maple, basswood, beech, birch, elm, &c.

SCENERY.

The scenery is varied, and in many instances extremely grand. At Beaver Creek, about 9 miles north of Washago, the rocks rise almost perpendicular near 200 feet, from the loftiest peak of which a deer, being closely pursued, is said to have leaped down in safety to the valley below and thereby escaped.

MUSKOKA LAKE

Is one of the most charming sheets of water in this Province. There are over 300 Islands dotting its surface, which, for beauty and variety, cannot be excelled. That portion of the Lake between Gravenhurst and the Narrows is exceedingly beautiful, and much admired by the lovers of nature. Mrs. John B. Robinson, Mrs. Dodge, and other ladies who have travelled extensively, pronounce the scenery to be equal to anything to be found on this continent.

THE MUSKOKA RIVER

Is very attractive and celebrated for the perfect reflection which is everywhere noticeable—in fact, some declare that in this respect it is equal to the far-famed Lakes of Killarney.

The *Telegraph* says:—

"LAKE ROSSEAU

Is perhaps the most beautiful of the chain of water communication. It is particularly placid, filled with picturesque islands, and the shores are wooded to the water's edge. In its general characteristics, it greatly resembles the celebrated Lakes of Killarney. The party landed at the head of the sheet of water, at a place named Sandy Cut, but which, before the party left, was duly christened Port Sandfield, in honor of the Hon. J.S. Macdonald."

The Rev. Mr. Rogers, Presbyterian Minister, writes in the *Record* for January, 1871, that "This Lake is a perfect gem of beauty, about 12 miles by 7, variegated by numerous islands, a place fit for a philosopher's musing or a poet's fancy. This Lake will soon be connected with Lake Joseph by a short canal, a lake of larger dimensions and much spoken of for its lovely and variegated scenery. It is also being connected in the same way to Lake Muskoka at Port Carling."

Speaking of Lake Muskoka, he says:—"The scenery on this Lake is unsurpassed by anything I have seen in the Dominion."

LAKE ST. JOSEPH.

This is a large and beautiful sheet of water connecting with Lake Rosseau at Port Sandfield. The land adjoining this Lake is principally timbered with hardwood and of very superior quality; at one point it touches very close upon the Georgian Bay, where a shipping port and town will in all probability shortly spring up; true, there are other parts where they have less rock and can boast of better farming country; but there is no spot more healthy or romantic than this. Here the sportsman and the pleasure-seeker can enjoy the richest possible treat, and men with shattered constitutions may here have them repaired. Ye broken-down millionaires, fly hither and recuperate!

The Rev. Alex. Kennedy, of Pickering, writes under date 21st Dec., 1870:—

"My intercourse with settlers, whether village or landward, gave me a highly favourable opinion of their intelligence, energy, self-reliance, and contentment. I do trust that, by diligent effort and sobriety, they will win for themselves prosperity in their forest homes. Of the soil and climate of the country my very limited knowledge forbids me to speak dogmatically; but, from what I saw and learned, my conviction is that both are better than your rocky southern entrance and your northern latitude would lead a stranger to infer. But of your lake scenery I feel free to speak in the highest terms. It has been my lot to see many corners of creation in several and distant lands; but, for romantic grandeur, I am not sure that I have seen anything to surpass Lake Muskoka, with its all but countless islands and its rocky and wooded shores. Without much hazard of prophetic failure, the day may be predicted, and not far distant either, when the wealthy in our large cities will erect villas for the summer residence of their families on the healthful and enchanting shores of Lake Muskoka."

THE CROPS.

Splendid samples of wheat have been raised in the district, the yield being large and the grain of superior quality. From practical experience the writer feels confident that, by good tillage and by paying proper attention to the rotation of crops, this staple can be profitably raised. Oats grow luxuriantly and pay well, we have seen as good oats here as we ever beheld either in Ireland or Scotland, and recommend Scotchmen in particular to make Muskoka their home, for they will be certain to have an abundance of oat-cake and porridge.

Indian corn does well in some localities. It has been successfully raised by the Indians since they can remember.

Great crops of potatoes and turnips are also raised, and of the very best quality. Vegetables of all kinds do well. Apple trees, berry-bushes and all descriptions of fruit-bearing plants seem to do well. Clover and all the grasses are eminently successful even on the ridges; such a thing as burnt-up pastures being almost unknown, the herbage being green and fresh from early spring till snow falls again in the autumn. In a warm and well-watered country like this, crops can be raised on soil that would be useless if subject to drought.

Mr. Walter Sharp, of lots number 4 and 5 in the 13th concession of the Township of Draper, had 15 acres last year under oats, which yielded 900 bushels, or 60 bushels to the acre.

Mr. Andrew Thompson, Postmaster at Uffington, in the Township of Draper, and District of Muskoka, planted an early rose potatoe weighing one and three quarter ounces, and raised from the same sixteen and three-quarter pounds, thus yielding 153 times the quantity planted.

The Rev. Mr. Rogers, Presbyterian minister, states in the *Record* for January, 1871.

"The crops this year (1870) are excellent. I saw fields of oats that would yield 50 bushels per acre, also very good samples of wheat and the best potatoes I have ever tasted. I saw also many patches of Indian corn, of excellent growth and fully matured, and ripe tomatoes in great abundance."

The following is from the *Northern Advocate*:

EARLY ROSE POTATOES.—The Rev. Mr. Hill, of Peninsula Farm, Chaffey Township, planted two pounds of early rose potatoes, which yielded 224¾ pounds. At this rate an acre would produce between 1100 and 1200 bushels. We place Muskoka against any county in Ontario for potatoes.

WATER MELONS.—We have to thank Mr. Jacob Spence of the township of Draper for a valuable present of superior water melons just received. It was once thought that melons would not ripen here, but this season has demonstrated that they can be raised, and that the quality is equal to any grown in Ontario.

From the Report of the Commissioner of Agriculture and Public Works for 1870.

"I am glad to learn that most of those who have settled on the free grant lands seem to be satisfied with their choice. The excellent samples of wheat, oats, peas, &c., that were sent to my Department from the neighborhood of Bracebridge, which did not arrive in time for the Provincial Exhibition, clearly indicate the agricultural capabilities of the Muskoka District, which, with other extensive areas of fertile land in the course of being opened up to settlement in this Province, would afford homes of peace and plenty to thousands of industrious families in the mother country, that are now struggling with disappointment and want.

"Respectfully submitted,
"JOHN CARLING,
"*Commissioner.*

"TORONTO, January, 1871."

ROADS.

The prosperity of a country very much depends on the state of the roads, and speed and cheapness in travelling have a great deal to do with commercial success. This fact has been long recognized, and many improvements have been made in order to secure this most desirable end. Half a century ago, Macadam introduced his system which formed a new era in road making; and, while we cannot boast of having advanced so far as to have much macadamized road, still we are highly favored beyond many settlers of former days. By the introduction of ditching along the sides of the roads and elevating the centres, vast improvements have been made; and the settlers have no cause to complain, as the Government have done nobly in this respect.

The road from Washago to Muskoka Falls was commenced in 1858; again in 1864 the Government expended a large sum of money in doing repairs, when detours were made at Hock-rock and Golden Creek, which not only improved the road but added very much to the comfort of the settlers. In 1866, repairs were made on the Peterson Road (running through Draper) under the efficient superintendence of Mr. Oliver, whose engineering ability was ably manifested in the improvements which he introduced.

In 1866 the Parry Sound Road was completed, thereby connecting Lake Couchiching with the Georgian Bay at Parry Sound Harbor—a distance of 80 miles; since then the Government have pushed road-making through with vigor. A good plank and gravel road has been built between Washago and Gravenhurst, which is a great boon to the settlers. The Stevenson Road has also been extended and bridges built, thereby opening up a large section of good country. The Nipissing Road has also been opened up to the Maganetawan, and rapid improvements are still going on.

PROGRESS.

It is a satisfaction to find that, with the confederation of the Provinces, some life has been thrown into this movement, and a deeper interest is taken in the matter; but it is only of late that this subject has met with that attention which it deserves.

The results of the past two years have been most encouraging, and warrant increasing exertions in this important department. The Hon. John Carling deserves the highest praise for the course he has pursued. He has done all that could reasonably be expected, and has shown himself to be "the right man in the right place;" and, from the opportunities which the different members of the Government have had of judging of the success of those immigrants who have settled in this district, I feel confident that they will be prepared to lend every assistance in their power to promote a scheme which is so good for individuals, and beneficial for the state.

It cannot be said that there has been a great rush at any time, still the settlement has made sure and steady progress, every year having added to its population and development. Morrison Township, the first through which you pass on entering the territory, possesses considerable good land, although it is rough and rocky through that part penetrated by the Colonization Road; still west of that and in the neighborhood of Sparrow Lake the soil is rich and the per centage of agricultural land large; hence it has been settled by a very intelligent and industrious class of inhabitants; schools and churches have been erected, mills and post-offices have been established, and the settlers begin to feel that brighter days await them.

Muskoka Township, to the north of Morrison, has participated largely of the spirit of enterprise which has everywhere characterized the settlement of this District. It can boast of Gravenhurst, a spirited and ambitious village, the centre of large lumbering operations, where the principal part of the steam boat building of the north is carried on. This township contains a large number of settlers, including not only the industrious poor, but men of position and wealth. A.J. Alport, Esq., J.P., of Maple Grove, has his home here. Wonderful improvements have been made in this township; large clearances have been affected, and everything indicates great prosperity and perfect contentment.

Draper Township has not been lacking in that energy which has so strongly marked the history of the Muskoka Territory. The enterprise manifested by the two first settlers, Mr. Donald Ferguson (a Highland Scotchman), and the author, who is a Lowland Scotchman, has been largely imbibed by all who have succeeded them, so that the development has been most rapid, as will be seen by a reference to the statistics furnished in another part of this work. One serious drawback to the settlement of this Township has been the difficulty of getting to the land on the north side of the Muskoka River. However, notwithstanding this hinderance, a large number of settlers have lately found their way thither, and the number is constantly increasing.

The soil is very superior, and as bridges will shortly be built, it is reasonable to expect that very soon all the unoccupied lots will be taken up.

Macaulay Township has great natural advantages, and is admirably situated. The head of navigation on the north branch of the Muskoka River, where the thriving village of Bracebridge now stands, touches the south-west corner of the Township. The soil is good, and settlers are rapidly filling up the Township. Settlement is progressing most favorably, the prospects are good, and Macaulay is destined to become one of the richest Townships in the District.

Stephenson Township has made great headway during the past year; hundreds of settlers have been induced to take up land there, so that it now compares favorably with any in this section.

The settlers are improving in their circumstances; and not only can they live, but many of them are saving money.

Monck Township is very conveniently situated to the west of Macaulay; it also is advancing with sure and steady pace; no one, in passing through this District, can fail to notice that the settlers do not believe in standing still; for, wherever you go, progress and rapid improvement are observable.

Watt Township has settled up quickly and the inhabitants are noted for their intelligence and perseverance; new frame houses are taking place of the old log cabins, and everything gives evidence of prosperity and success. Besides those already enumerated, the Townships of McLean, Brunel, Stisted, Chaffey, Cardwell, Wood and Medora, are filling up rapidly, and the accounts received from those who have located there are most favourable.

In 1868, Muskoka was organized into a Territorial District, and a Stipendiary Magistrate was appointed; the Crown Land Agency then became an appendage to that office, Mr. C.W. Lount receiving the appointment.

As an evidence of the growth of the settlement, I may just state that, according to the Crown Lands Reports, only 163 persons located on wild lands in 1864; whilst the Hon. John Carling stated in the House of Assembly, on the 9th of December, 1870, that no less than 139,000 acres of land had been taken up during that year in the Muskoka District alone, and I may add that the past success of the settlement is a sufficient guarantee to all who shall hereafter locate, that, with sobriety, industry and perseverance, they may succeed.

The following statistics will enable the reader to mark the steady progress which the settlement is making. I submit the Townships of Draper, Macaulay and Stephenson, simply from the fact that I was Reeve of said Municipality.

THE "NIPISSING," A NEW STEAMER.

The "Wenonah" has done good service to the settlers in the Muskoka district during the past few years; while at the same time she has proved remunerative to her enterprising proprietor, and I rejoice that she has fostered a trade upon these lakes, which necessitates the construction of a much larger vessel. I have thought that a description of the *new steamer* at present building at Gravenhurst, would interest my readers, and have therefore gleaned the following particulars, which will give some idea of what she will be like when finished;—Her length of keel will be 115 feet; length of deck, 123 feet; breadth of beam, 19 feet; breadth over all, 31 feet; gross tonnage, 150 tons. She will be driven by a low pressure beam engine, manufactured by Messrs. F.G. Becket & Co., of Hamilton. The length of stroke will be six feet; the bore of cylinder, 24 inches. Her boiler will be a return tubular made of ⅜ inch Low-moor plate, weighing 8½ tons. The whole construction of this steamer is under the supervision of one of the most experienced mechanical engineers and draftsmen in the Dominion. The contractor is Thomas Walters, Esq. The master builder is Mr. Robert Robin-

United Townships of Draper, Macaulay, Stephenson, Ryde and Oakley.

RECAPITULATION.

	1868.			1869.				1870.			
	Draper.	Macaulay.	Stephenson.	Draper.	Macaulay.	Stephenson.	Oakley.	Draper.	Macaulay.	Stephenson.	Oakley.
Number of ratepayers	71	63	55	86	80	87	7	101	143	127	8
Number of acres resident	8,647	7,107	6,760	13,034	9,093	12,367	900	17,542	18,192	18,687	1,700
Number of acres cleared	664	487	354	928	504	416	109	1,010	713	468	
Number of acres non-resident	3,800	850	1,100	700	400	700	600	1,000	100		102
Total no. of acres resident and non-resident	12,447	6,705	7,860	13,734	9,493	13,067	1,500	18,542	18,292	18,687	1,700
Value of resident lands	14,800	15,595	8,375	17,020	5,388	11,015	3,000	20,344	25,101	16,325	2,400
Value of non-resident lands	2,280	550	550	1,075	375	575	300	850	100		
Total value of resident and non-resident lands	17,080	16,145	8,925	18,045	5,763	11,590	3,300	21,194	25,101	16,325	3,400
Value personal property	1,900	2,650	400	2,500	4,950	400	3,200	2,150	5,600	900	3,400
Total value real and personal property and taxable income	17,700	18,245	8,775	19,520	21,338	11,415	6,200	22,477	30,700	17,227	6,600
Number of persons in family of persons rated	292	202	165	363	247	233	12	352	481	337	25
Number of cattle	147	96	50	170	97	70	5	201	133	114	6
Number of sheep	64	38	30	93	29	27		88	35	33	
Number of hogs	37	21	9	10	14	4		10	26	7	2
Number of horses	15	3		18	10	3		16	20	4	

son, of Kingston; and, all things considered, I feel justified in stating that she will be a model of design, comfort and beauty, being the exact copy of the "Emily May" in every particular, only one-sixth smaller. She is to be fitted up as a *mail*, *express*, and passenger steamer. The latest improvements will be adopted in the build of her decks, cabin and general outfit; and she will be furnished in the most elegant manner, so as to promote the comfort of those who shall sail in her over our beautiful lakes. Her average speed will be 14 miles an hour, and she is expected to be launched on the 15th of April next. I certainly must congratulate the inhabitants of this district upon the improved accommodation furnished; while at the same time I wish Mr. A.P. Cockburn success in his grand enterprise.

VILLAGES.

As the settlement fills up, Villages arise as a natural consequence. The following sketches will no doubt prove that the District is in a prosperous state:—

BRACEBRIDGE.

The village of Bracebridge is the most important in the District of Muskoka; it is situated in the south-west portion of the Township of Macaulay, 11 miles north of Gravenhurst, on the north branch of the Muskoka River, at what is known as the North Falls, about 5 miles from its influx with Lake Muskoka. When the writer first visited Muskoka, in 1861, there was not a tree cut nor a settler to be found on the present site—all was a dense forest; in fact, there was no road to it, and the only means of crossing the River was by walking over a pine log which fortunately spanned the stream, which I can assure you was a dangerous experiment. What a change has taken place since then! While I write, a hundred chimneys are sending forth their smoke and scores of teams are driving past, giving evidence of activity and life. There are 4 large hotels, 7 excellent stores, 2 saw-mills, grist-mill, 2 bakers' shops, 2 butchers' shops, 2 boot stores, carpenters' shops, sash and door factory, blacksmith shops, cabinet warehouse, drug store, book store, Court-house, Crown Lands office, Registry office, Jail, Printing office, Churches, Schools, &c., Orange Hall, Post-office with daily mail, money order office, and P.O. Savings Bank. Passengers can, during navigation, come through from Toronto in a day. Bracebridge is destined to become a town of great importance, situated as it is in the centre of the District, surrounded by a rich farming country, with numberless avenues all leading directly to it; and, being on the route of the Toronto, Simcoe and Muskoka Junction Railway, it cannot fail to keep the lead, as it has already taken it.

Bracebridge is now certain of being made the present terminus of the T.S. & M.J. Railway. The Government has placed it upon the list of those lines entitled to aid, and has granted $4,000 a mile towards its construction from Washago. The Company, anxious to penetrate the back settlements, have pledged themselves, on the Townships giving a bonus of $50,000, to construct the Road with all possible speed.

This village at present is a more important place than Orillia was ten years ago, and the commercial position of this village in 1871 far exceeds the standing of that village in 1861; and, if the past can be an index to the future, we shall gain more during the coming five than it has in the past ten.

A SHORT SKETCH OF THE RISE AND PROGRESS OF THE VILLAGE OF GRAVENHURST.

Ten years ago, the present site of the village of Gravenhurst was a wilderness of pines which flourished in all their primeval grandeur. But, as resources and advantages of the country became gradually known to the outside world, eager immigrants from the mother country and land seekers from the older settlements came here; amongst those Messrs. Jas. Sharp, senior; David Wright, Joseph Brock, Edward and James Hewitt, and Jas. McCabe, the last-named party also being proprietor of the "Free Masons Arms" Hotel. The progress of Gravenhurst and vicinity was necessarily slow for a few years.

Messrs. P. Cockburn & Son, commencing lumbering operations in the country during the winter of 1865-'66, gave an impetus to industry and advancement previously unknown; they purchased logs from the settlers and gave them employment during the winter months, soon convincing the inhabitants that pine trees were useful for other purposes than being burnt into ashes. Mr. A.P. Cockburn, M.P.P., contributed very materially about this time to the welfare and progress of the settlement by placing a steamer on Muskoka Lake, built near Gravenhurst wharf, and known as the "Wenonah;" he also opened a general store, distinguished as the "Montreal Store,"— since that the country has steadily progressed.

Gravenhurst is pleasantly situated on a gentle declivity between Muskoka Bay and Gull Lake; it is distant from Toronto, 106 miles; from Orillia, 26 miles; from Severn Bridge, 12 miles; and from Bracebridge, 11 miles. It is connected with Lake Couchiching by a new plank and gravel road constructed during the past summer. The principal buildings are Brown's hotel, Mr. Cooper's new building, the Queen's hotel, the stores of Messrs. Cockburn & Co. and George Clarke, the Episcopalian Church. Messrs. Sibbald & Chamberland are building an extensive saw mill; a planing machine and sash and door factory are also to be run in connexion with the saw-mill.

A.P. Cockburn, Esq., is constructing a fine new steamer on Muskoka Bay, which he expects to launch in the month of April next. I might mention that James Sharp, senior, is general agent for the different steamers and the "Union Line" at Gravenhurst. The lumbering firm of Hotchkiss, Hughson & Co. have an office at this point. The only places of worship at present are the

English Church and school-house. Two new churches and a public hall are in contemplation. The medical profession is represented by Dr. J. Adams, of Nova Scotia. Amongst the expectations are the Toronto, Simcoe and Muskoka Junction Railway, and a branch of the Montreal Telegraph Line. Being situated at the foot of navigation, Gravenhurst does a large and increasing trade. The steamer *Wenonah* calls at the wharf twice each day. The village is favored with a daily mail, with a through mail from Toronto during the season of navigation.

"SEVERN BRIDGE"

This part of Morrison was first settled about 1858. The first settlers were James H. Jackson, William Johnston, and John Young. It was then the farthest point north that was settled. The next season five or six families more came in among them, the Messrs. Symingtons and a few families of Prussians. The first store was owned by O'Brien & Co., of Orillia, in the house now occupied by Mr. Mackenzie as an hotel. The next store was kept by a Mr. Gray, and H.W. Dillon opened a tavern. There is a good plank road, splendid water privilege, a first class hotel, two excellent stores, one kept by Mr. Jackson, the other by Mr. Samuel R. Thomson, who has named that part of "Severn Bridge" Sandy Row, in honor of that loyal part of Belfast, Ireland; they are first class stores and reflect credit on the enterprising proprietors. There is also a Town hall, Orange hall, blacksmith's shop, and carpenter's, and wood-turner's shop. A new bridge has been built this season by Government, under the able superintendence of W.L. Owen, Esq., and it is said to be one of the best got up bridges north of Toronto. Severn Bridge is two miles north of Washago and is very rocky immediately at "Sandy Row," but there is a great deal of good land in Morrison and the adjoining townships. Two miles up the Severn River are the falls; these are beautifully picturesque, and will repay tourists for their trouble in visiting the same. Four miles down the river are Grass and Sparrow Lakes, justly famed for their fisheries. There are some Prussians around Sparrow Lake, and the other settlers are a mixture of Irish and Scotch. The settlers in Morrison are noted for their loyalty.

WASHAGO

Is the little village at the head of navigation, on Lake Couchiching, 12 miles north of Orillia, and forms the entrance to the Free Grant district of Muskoka. Here the steamboats land their freight and passengers. It contains an hotel, post office, and saw mill. Many have turned back on their arrival here, and it is not much to be wondered at, for the scene is anything but inviting. Rock is very prominent, but I assure my readers that if they will penetrate the settlement, a more pleasing prospect will meet their view.

MUSKOKA FALLS.

Muskoka Falls is situated on the north-west corner of the Township of Draper, at the junction of the Peterson line of road with the Muskoka Road. It is 21 miles north of Washago, and 3 miles south of Bracebridge. There is in this village a post office, with daily mail; store, hotel, school, meeting-house, &c. The soil in the neighbourhood is good, and the country around is well settled. It is chiefly remarkable for the beauty of its scenery. The Grand Muskoka Falls are always attractive to tourists, and much admired by the lovers of nature. In the spring of 1866 a scene of unusual interest presented itself. In former years the spray had formed an arch over the Falls, but on this occasion it assumed the form of a cone with a crater, and from its mouth the spray came boiling forth in awful grandeur, ascending at least 100 feet. It might be compared to a mighty, massive silver fountain, sending forth its sparkling waters. Any one who has witnessed Vesuvius burning in his fury may form some conception of this grand sight. As I gazed upon the scene a double rainbow spanned the Falls; countless icicles were hanging from the branches of the tall pines as they bent gracefully over the cataract, and I wished that the world might be privileged with the sight. I drove some distance in order to get an artist to take a negative, but the spray was so great that a good picture could not be obtained. Multitudes of those who love the sublime and picturesque take a trip hither once a year; and, when we consider that the Falls are 175 in height, and that 3,670 tons of water per minute rush through this narrow mountain gorge and descend to the basin beneath with a voice like thunder, it is not to be wondered at that visitors from almost every part of the continent have carved their names on the bridge that spans the Grand Muskoka Falls. The writer is not a little proud of the thought that he was one of the first to carve his name on that wonderful record.

MUSKOKA.

Here hoary rocks that countless ages past
Have brav'd the force of winter's wildest blast,
And scorching heat of summer's fiercest ray,
Those rugged, beetling crags of granite gray,
With awful majesty, sublimely grand,
In all their native, ancient, moss-clad glory stand.

Behold the maple groves in bright array,
Their gorgeous tints and brilliant hues display.
Among their short-liv'd fading glories see,
Emblem of constancy, the hemlock tree,—
That ever green its spreading branches show,
Alike in summer's sultry heat and winter's chilling snow.

Above the hemlocks green and maples bright,
The sombre pine uplifts its stately height—
Its cone-capp'd head above the other trees.
Its tassel'd foliage trembles in each breeze,
And nimble red squirrels sport and wild birds sing
Among the waving branches of the forest king.

The wild duck skims along the glassy lake,
The wild hare fearless plays among the brake;
In glens where foot of white man ne'er hath trode,
The shaggy bear and fox make their abode;
And through the vastness of their forest home,
The graceful bounding deer and savage wild wolf roam.

The calm, unruffled river quiet flows,
Save when some sudden breeze mars its repose,
Or when some scaly tenant of the flood
Darts forth his shiny length in quest of food;
Or o'er its smooth and placid surface glides
The fragile bark canoe the skilfull Indian guides.

But see now, bursting through the narrow gorge—
Its wildly rushing torrent seethe and surge,
One boiling mass of foam, from rock to rock,—
It falls, it bounds, with quick successive shock.
The thundering noise the rocky banks resound,
And waken countless forest echoes far around.

The rocks toss up the foam in sportive play,
And glittering rainbows sparkle in the spray;
The awful scene, the deaf'ning roar appals—
Sublime, majestic, Grand Muskoka Falls!
That mock the puny arts of man, and stand,
The wondrous mighty work of an Almighty hand.

But more, the scenery sublime and grand:
See yonder, where the stalwart chopper's hand
Has fell'd the woods and cleared the trees away,
And fruitful crops his labor well repay.
The seed he sows a plenteous increase bear,
And well-filled granaries reward his prudent care.

See through yon field, how patiently and slow
The meekly lab'ring, well-fed oxen go,
And pull the plough to break the fertile soil
That yields rich harvest for the settler's toil;
Or homeward draw the heavy loaded wain,
To fill the bursting barns with sheaves of golden grain.

GRAND MUSKOKA FALLS.

A happy home where peace and plenty dwell,
And ruddy cheeks of health and comfort tell;
And while they robust, vig'rous strength enjoy,
In useful tasks the working hours employ.
With pleasures true and real contentment blest,
And honest labor makes thrice welcome evening's rest.

Draper, 1869.

Muskoka is a transformation of the Indian word Musquoto, signifying clear sky, or no clouds. Intelligent Indians inform us that Musquoto was the first Indian who discovered Muskoka Lake and River, and that they took the name of Musquoto from this fact; and, by some transformation on the part of the whites, Musquoto has been transformed into Muskoka.

PORT CARLING.

This thriving village is situated in the Township of Medora, on the banks of the Biasong (Thunder lightning) river, on both sides of the rapids from whence the river derives its name. The village has been named in honor of the Hon. John Carling, through whose practical knowledge of and well-known interest in the improvement of the route of communication with the Free Grant District, a Lock is in course of construction to enable our line of steamboats during the season of navigation to traverse the Muskoka, Rosseau, and Joseph Lakes. This lock is in the centre of the village plot which has been surveyed, and will soon be in market, in lots of different sizes, for building purposes. These lots are well arranged and beautifully situated, sloping gently down to the river; some have a little rolling stone, but the majority are good clay loam and will prove a good investment to the purchaser. Already there are several houses, hotels and stores, doing a brisk business, so that intending settlers will be favorably circumstanced in fixing up in the bush. The land on Joseph Lake is remarkably good; and, as it is contiguous to the

Georgian Bay, a ready market for all produce will soon be within reach. To show the rapid progress of settlement in this delightful neighbourhood, I have only to mention that the first settler, Mr. Michael Bailey, came in to this place in June, 1865, and now there are scores of settlers all around and many more coming in. The traffic per steamer "Wenonah" has been as much as she could carry; and the "Wabamick," on Lake Rosseau, has had her capacity fully tested during the season of navigation just closed. Arrangements are being made for a school which will be in operation in a few days, so that educational privileges will be within reach of most. Religious services are held fortnightly by the Wesleyans from Bracebridge, and other ministers come occasionally. The Orangemen are about building a hall, which will be completed early in spring and be quite an ornament to the village and a great public benefit.

There is a post-office kept in the store of J.D. Cockburn, Esq., whose attention to that part of his business entitles him to great respect; and a Land and general commission office, under the superintendence of Mr. G.C. Hazlewood, who will be most happy to supply information to inquirers. A Colonization Road has been made, connecting Port Carling and Bracebridge, some eighteen miles distant, so that in summer and winter our channels of communication are good. Upon the whole, claims of this neighborhood upon the attention of intending settlers are great; and the fact of our having a daily mail in summer, and twice a week during the winter, supplies all that which such a new country could be expected to furnish.

PORT SANDFIELD.

This place is a cut made by Government to give steamboat communication between Rosseau and Joseph Lakes, and is named after the Honourable J. Sandfield Macdonald, Premier of our Local Legislature. The ceremony was duly performed by the Rev. A. Styleman Herring, B.A., London, England, during his trip into the Free Grant Territory in the summer of 1870. It is about three miles in a bee line to the west of Port Carling, and about five miles by water. It is every way likely that a village will rise up here of some importance.

ROSSEAU.

This village is at the head of Lake Rosseau, it contains a post-office, large summer hotel, and some stores.

NIPISSING JUNCTION.

This village is only about a mile distant from Rosseau, 22 miles from Parry Sound, and 32 miles from Bracebridge, at the junction of the Parry Sound and Nipissing Colonization Roads. Here there is a post-office named Ashdown, a large hotel kept by Mr. Richard Irwin and several good stores; there is also a blacksmith's shop, and the prospects of the place are cheering.

MAGANETAWA.

Maganetawa is situated half way between Rosseau Junction (at the head of Lake Rosseau), and Lake Nipissing, and is about 31 miles distant from both. James Miller, the first settler in this section, located here in October 1868, his nearest neighbour at that time resided at Rosseau Junction; his example has encouraged others to follow, and now there is a good settlement and considerable clearing, some having not less than 30 acres under cultivation. A village is just starting, and at this point a store and post-office are much wanted. Land seekers have now the advantage of a good colonization road, the soil is a good clay loam, and it is asserted by some that there is no less than 80 per cent of it fit for cultivation. There is a splendid water privilege here on which Mr. Miller is erecting a saw-mill; a good Sabbath-school is also kept up for the benefit of the children. I have no hesitation in stating that Maganetawa will yet be a place of considerable importance, its situation is excellent.

HUNTSVILLE.

Huntsville is situated on the Vernon River, near its mouth or confluence with the waters of Fairy Lake, in the Township of Chaffey. The Huntsville post-office was opened January, 1870. Two stores are now being built, with cheering prospects, on the part of the spirited proprietors, of doing a good business. The Muskoka Road has been extended to this place a few months ago, and a very substantial bridge spans the waters of the Vernon. Lakes Vernon, Fairy and Peninsula, are all beautiful sheets of water in this vicinity, abounding with a great variety of fish; while their sloping banks and beautiful forests have rendered them objects of delight to the admirers of rural scenery. The land in the vicinity of these Lakes is of a superior quality, which is being rapidly cleared of its timber; and waving fields of grain, with the most abundant crops of potatoes, &c., amply reward the enterprising settlers for their toil.

Maple, elm, basswood, hemlock, birch and iron wood, may be regarded as the prevailing kinds of timber. Pine is scarce, yet there are some fine specimens both of the white and Norway pine. The land is well watered by numerous springs and creeks; swamps are seldom found, while the old laurentian formation of rock, crops out on almost every lot of land; but this rock is not deceptive to the agriculturist, as he may dig or plough close beside the visible rock without obstruction. Hunters report much good land north and east of Franklin and Chaffey. The extension of the Muskoka Road to form a junction with the Bobcaygeon Road, on the east of Franklin, would be a great boon to this section of country. To effect this, a petition, numerously signed, has been forwarded to Parliament. The influx of settlers to the vicinity of these Lakes during last summer has been very great, yet there is much good land to be given away. Preparations are being made for the erection of churches and mills next summer.

EARLY REMINISCENCES.

THE RICE QUARREL.

In the early settlement of Draper, three families resided together until they would have time to erect a separate house for each. One of the women had brought in a quantity of rice, which mysteriously disappeared little by little; and, after having been robbed of her entire package, she gave expression to her suspicion that one or other of the women must have been interfering with the same; this gave rise to terrible quarrel, and made a wide breach in those three families; a separation took place, and considerable sensation was created.

After some time light was thrown upon the whole affair in the following manner:—one of the men cut down a hollow tree, and as he was cutting it up, you may judge his surprise as the rice came running out; the thief was at last detected; a naughty chipmonk or squirrel had found its way into the shanty, and as there happened to be a crack in the box which contained the rice, an entrance was effected, and little by little it removed the stock in order to complete its winter store, but the woodsman's axe blasted its hopes, cleared the innocent, and shamed the quarrellers.

WILD BEASTS.

No fear need be entertained with reference to wild animals; I have been in the settlement for about ten years, during which period not a single case of injury has occurred. The sight of a wild animal is very rare; shortly after I settled in Muskoka, as I was on my way to the Severn Bridge, I saw a large gray wolf; it was crossing the road near where James Boyd now lives, about a mile north of Grant's Mill; when it heard my footsteps, it stopped. I shall never forget how I felt as I looked for the first time upon this noble specimen of the North American wolf; there it stood about 20 yards off, with glaring eyes, pricked up ears, and bushy tail. After we looked at each other for a few seconds, it turned round and walked away in the direction from whence it came as cowardly as possible.

The wolves of Canada are not to be compared to those of Russia in ferocity; besides, deer are so abundant that they seldom know what hunger is. I have heard them howling as they were on the pursuit, and the sound is anything but pleasant.

The bear has been often seen, but has never been known to attack any one. They invariably flee from the face of man, and never give battle unless in defence of their young, to which they are strongly attached.

The lynx is very rare, only one having been shot in the District. As an evidence of the perfect safety which we enjoy, I may state that not so much as a lamb has been destroyed by any wild animals in this neighbourhood.

INDIANS.

Few Indians reside in the District, but numbers of them pass through it on their way from Rama to their hunting grounds. They are a very quiet, inoffensive people, fond of jewellery and gaudy attire. They sing very sweetly, and the squaws execute some nice bead work, which displays great taste. It is amusing to see them gliding along in their bark canoes. They are dying off very fast, and I fear that they will soon become extinct. Some of them, however, live to a good old age.

Old Chief Yellow-head died in 1865, aged 106 years. He was an honest Indian, much respected by all who knew him, and he continued to frequent his hunting grounds till a few days before his death. On his last trip he called at the residence of the writer, and remained over night.

LOST IN THE WOODS.

The following was written some years ago, on the occasion of
Moses Richardson and his wife getting lost in the woods;
Draper township was then but thinly settled, and the sensation
it created in the settlement was intense; I happened to be one of
the party who went in search of the missing ones. Persons unacquainted with the bush should be careful not to penetrate far
into it, unless provided with a compass. "What means this blow-
ing of horns, firing of arms, and the oft-repeated 'Hoop, whoo'
that greets the ear and arrests the attention of every settler?"
"A man and his wife are lost in the woods" is the prompt and
excited reply. How sad is every countenance, how agitated every
breast, how anxious every neighbour! The unhappy pair had
gone in search of their cattle, mistaken their way, and got lost in
the dense forest; with wild desperation they are forcing their
way through the thicket of the swamp, or ascending the rugged
mountain's brow, or climbing over logs vainly in search of the
home they left; but, alas, they are totally bewildered and every
step they take leads them farther from "The dearest spot on
earth," "Home, sweet home." The neighbours now begin to col-
lect from all points of the compass; they form themselves into
companies, and decide what the signal shall be in case the unhappy wanderers are found. Animated by a noble philanthropy
they start, cheered by the happy thought of saving the lost; for
hours they pursue their difficult task; crossing deep gullies,
ascending almost perpendicular heights, then going down steep
precipices, they onward go; the sun begins to sink in the western
sky, the shades of evening fall upon them, the dark curtains of
night at length are thrown around them; to proceed farther
would be folly; in the dark they might pass the objects of their
search; an eminence is sought and a fire is kindled, in order to
attract the notice of the lost ones; the searchers gather round it;
a little bread and pork, with some "bright water" from the brook

that flows at the mountain's base, form their evening meal; no
levity characterizes their conduct; there is but one expression
visible on each countenance, and that is sadness; hemlock brush
is cut and spread that the weary searchers may rest themselves
thereon; sleep is out of the question; their trouble is too deep for
them to enjoy "Nature's sweet restorer, balmy sleep." The
solemn words, "Let us pray," for the first time are repeated in
this dense forest; and, on the still evening air, prayer ascends to
Him who came "to save that which was lost." Here, many miles
from any human habitation, prayer for the first time is offered
by "white men" to "The Great Spirit;" the missing ones are not
forgotten, and earnest supplication is made that God would
direct their steps. But what of the poor wanderers?—they are
weak and faint; hunger drives them to despair and death; death
from starvation stares them in the face; the husband, as the only
alternative, urges his wife to cut a slice from the calf of his leg in
order to satiate her craving for food; but the faithful wife repu-
diated the thought, and replied that she would rather willingly
die with her husband.

Moments of anxiety pass, and the long-looked for morning
dawns, the sun begins to peep in the eastern horizon, and after
partaking of some refreshment they again start on their mission
of humanity; the burning sun beams upon them, they wipe the
perspiration from their brows, and the flies from off their necks,
and uncomplainingly persevere over logs and swamps; now the
coat of one of the party is caught on a snag and rent to shivers,
while another man's pants are almost torn from top to bottom.
Hark! Hark! The report of firearms informs them of the fact
that one of the companies has found the wanderers, all fire off
their guns in ecstasy and run in the direction of the firing to
catch a glimpse of "Moses" and his wife. Oh! what a sad sight
was then presented to their gaze. Poor creatures, how sad their
condition, how weak, how changed, what wildness is in their
eyes; they are mad with fright, and are starving with hunger, as

one pipe of tobacco has been all that they have enjoyed for over 48 hours; the realization that they were lost, the fear of death, and the lashings of a guilty conscience for having gone out on the Sabbath-day in search of their cattle (they had been lost once before by disregarding the sacred precept "Remember the Sabbath-day to keep it holy"), together with their swollen limbs and bleeding forms, completed their misery and made the sight painful to behold; still there was joy mingled with sadness, every eye sparkles with delight, every countenance is lit up with a smile, all share in the triumph, men embrace each other and weep for gladness, while the forest rings with their shoutings and rejoicings. A little nourishment having been administered to the sufferers, the friends form themselves in procession and take turn in carrying the weak ones home; after reaching the log cabin and bidding them an affectionate farewell, they turn their steps homewards without a murmur, although they have travelled many weary miles, scorched by a burning sun, and as they proceed they inform every one they meet of the "Good news." "They're found, they're found!" is the repeated ejaculation, and all join in a sincere and hearty "thank God, thank God."

WHAT BROUGHT THE WRITER TO MUSKOKA.

The question has often been asked, What brought you to Canada?—and how did you find out about Muskoka? With reference to the first part of the enquiry, I have to state that having a numerous family, we commenced to consider what was best to be done under such circumstances. With our limited means we saw no prospect of ever being able to procure farms for them at home, so the thought of emigrating began to occupy our attention. With regard to the second, I would state that the Government, in 1861, sent Mr. J.A. Donaldson over to Great Britain and Ireland, in order to make Canada known, and promote emigration to the Provinces. It was announced in the

Belfast papers that he was staying at the "Plough Hotel," and would be glad to give advice to any who were desirous of emigrating to Canada. I waited upon him, and received a pamphlet, with map of Ontario, together with much valuable information. In looking over the map, I was favourably impressed with the position of Muskoka. Its proximity to Toronto, and its unlimited water facilities, led me to conclude that if the soil was what the surveyors reported it to be, that eventually it must become a place of considerable importance. On the 10th of May, 1861, we set sail from Londonderry, and arrived at Quebec on the 20th, after a pleasant voyage of ten days.

On passing along the Grand Trunk, I was very much disheartened at the appearance of the country; but as we neared Toronto the scene improved, and I thought Canada was not so bad a place after all. On our arrival in Toronto, I rented a house for a month for my family, while I proceeded to examine the Free Grant Lands of Muskoka. At Orillia many persons tried to dissuade me from going there. One man said, "If you go there you will die, and there will be no one to bury you;" but nothing daunted, I proceeded on my journey. On arriving at McCabe's Tavern, where the Village of Gravenhurst now stands, I hired a flat-bottomed boat, and rowed across Muskoka Lake, and up Muskoka River to the North Falls, now known as the Village of Bracebridge, which is the centre of the District. Here I was welcomed by Mr. James Cooper, to whom I had a note of introduction from R.J. Oliver, Esq., the Crown Lands Agent. After spending a night at the camp, near where the wharf now stands, I proceeded to Draper, and met with Mr. Richard Hanna, who was employed by the Government in opening up the Peterson Line of Road, who rendered me all the service in his power, and to whom I feel much indebted. After examining the land pretty thoroughly, I selected 400 acres on the banks of the south branch of the Muskoka River, about two miles east of the Grand Muskoka Falls, and succeeded in getting Mr. Hanna to quit road making, and fall to and chop ten acres of land, and build a log house, all of which he promised to have finished in a month, with the assistance of his men. I then went back to Toronto for my family, and, at the expiration of the month, returned, expecting that my house would be finished; but, while the frame was erected, it was destitute of floors and roof; so we were obliged to make a shake-down, with nothing but the blue canopy of Heaven for our covering. On retiring to rest all was pleasant, but at midnight the clouds began to gather, the lightning played, the thunder rolled, and the rain descended in torrents. There we were—out in the wild woods, miles from a human habitation. Moments of eternal duration passed away, and at last the morning came, when we got changes from our chests, and a fire started. This was our introduction to backwoods life. The news soon spread that we had located at Draper Falls, and others soon followed. The settlement has gone on increasing, until now the Township is well settled by a loyal and industrious people. Settlers now can form no estimate of the superior advantages which they have over the early settlers. When the writer first located, he had to float over streams on rafts, was obliged to go 35 miles to the mill; his nearest post office was 21 miles off, and he was destitute of stores, schools and churches, all of which the settlers now possess in abundance. In fact, such has been the rapid growth and development of the District that the writer could not imagine that half a century could possibly accomplish what has been achieved in a few years. It is truly astonishing how quickly forest becomes cleared.

> "The rising hut of logs prepared with skill,
>   Beside the shelter of some neighboring hill,
>   The "settler's home, of rude construction, stands,
>   The quick achievement of the neighboring hands.
>   Its sloping roof, of plank or shingle form,
>   Defies the dashes of the downward storm;

Rude as it seems to the fastidious eye,
Is still a home where many comforts lie,
Where humble worth can rest from healthful toil,
And eat the products of the generous soil;
Where female charms and virtues can expand
Beside the bounties of the well-cleared land,
And honest labor independence win,
Far from the haunts of idleness and sin."

I must say that several things impressed me very much on my arrival in this country; the first was the vast extent of Canada, the enormous area covered with woods and forest, its great lakes and noble rivers. Another thing that arrested my attention was, the advancement which it had made—Toronto, as regards buildings, business and beauty, being superior to many old country towns. I also noticed that, while the birds here are decked in gaudier colors than at home, yet they are very deficient in song. The improved position of the labouring classes was also very striking; working men are not only better paid here, but they have better fare; in this respect they enjoy perfect equality with their employers, eating at the same table, and treated in every way as equals.

HINTS TO EMIGRANTS.

THE BEST TIME TO ARRIVE.

If possible, get to the Free Grant District by the first of May. In order to get a little crop in, it is desirable that emigrants get here as early as possible. One week will be required to select your location, another to erect a log house; then follows the clearing of some land and cropping the same. It is not to be expected that much can be done the first season; but, by a little exertion, sufficient roots and vegetables may be grown for family use, and even some oats and peas may be raised. The writer has sown grain crops and planted potatoes as late as the last of June, and had a good return; but I prefer the month of May. Old country people have no idea of the rapidity with which crops mature in this country, especially in new land.

ON LEAVING HOME.

Emigrants are often induced to make a clean sweep and part with almost everything they possess. It is urged, as a reason for this course, that the freight is so high that the cost would overcome the profit. Now, there are many little necessaries, which, when sold, realize very little; while those same articles, if kept would be exceedingly valuable in the bush and prove a source of much comfort and convenience to the family as well; therefore, do not sacrifice your conveniences; they will not take up much room, and the freight is nothing in comparison with the comfort they will confer. Remember to bring all your bedding and apparel with you.

THE PASSAGE.

Provide yourselves with some fresh eggs packed in salt, a piece of smoked ham, a few pounds of cheese, some pickles; and, if you are Scotch, a quantity of oatmeal cake. Put these articles, together with any other little conveniences, in a trunk which you will keep beside you in your berth. All your boxes and luggage will be stowed away in the hold of the vessel; so, whatever you absolutely require on the voyage, should be put in this trunk, which you will keep in your berth room; it will also serve as a seat.

MAKE FOR TORONTO,

The capital of the Province of Ontario, the business centre and seat of commerce. The Free Grant Districts of Parry Sound and Muskoka are reached from it. On your arrival in the city, inquire for Mr. John A. Donaldson, Government Emigration Agent, who will give all necessary information.

A HOME IN THE WILD WOODS.

Having made up your minds to take advantage of the Free Grants of land, lose no time but proceed without delay.

We have known some who, on their arrival, frittered away their means and time in our cities, and then, when their money was all gone, would make for the bush. Shun such folly, and do not delay a day; remember "time is money," and you will require every shilling you have to enable you to clear your farm and to keep you till you raise some crops, so do not waste a penny. On your arrival procure lists of the unoccupied lots and make a thorough examination of the land before locating; this is of great importance; your choice is for life, and your success or otherwise depends to a great extent upon the choice you make. There is an abundance of good land to choose from. Some take almost the first lot they see, without proper examination, and after a time get discouraged. The plan is to take time, in the first instance, and make a wise selection, then begin and work with a will.

The following is from the "Muskoka Settler's Guide:"

The class of settlers best adapted for the country are strong able men who will not be discouraged at every little incident they meet; men who have both vigour and courage to grapple with and overcome difficulties; men willing to live bare, work hard, and put up with many inconveniences for a few years. At the same time it must be observed that there have not yet, and humanly speaking never will be, such hardships encountered in this settlement as have been known in many others. There is the good Colonization Road, there are the mills and stores, and there is employment to be got at good wages. These are great advantages; still, there is the land to clear and fence, houses and barns to build, and roads to make, and any one coming here and expecting to find all the conveniences of an old settlement will be disappointed. Those, on the other hand, who are willing to economize and work hard for a few years may expect to see their labor crowned with success and to obtain and enjoy all the comforts of life in houses of their own. Many have come here with only a few dollars and have got on wonderfully, but not without losing much valuable time while working from home. A single man, or one with a very small family, might make a commencement with very little means. But to get oxen, a cow, feed, seed, and provisions, one would require to have something like $500 or £100 sterling, with which properly managed he will have every prospect of success. Many, however, have gone into the woods with only an axe and a will to use it and have been quite successful. In a new settlement there are always persons willing to sell out for the purpose of raising a little money to enable them to make a better start on another lot, and generally it will be best for those who have sufficient means and not much experience to buy some partly improved place. Lots with from 10 to 20 acres cleared may be got from $300 to $1000 according to quality of land and situation. In some localities lots with a few acres cleared can be obtained for less. Men thinking of coming into the bush should consider well before making a move. If they can do as well elsewhere they should not come here, and similarly those who can benefit themselves by leaving should lose no time in doing so. There may be some here who should never have come; but there are many who are not here who should be here. Those who have land and comfortable homes of their own should stay where they are; but there are many on small farms, on rented farms, and on mortgaged farms, with families of boys growing up, who could here secure homes both for themselves and their sons—many strong men who are hired out and working hard, who, if they would come here and *work as hard for themselves*, would soon be independent. There are many able-bodied men living in cities, paying high prices for provisions, house-rent, and fire-wood, and losing their health into the bargain, who here would get land of their own for nothing, a house of their own for the raising, firewood for the chopping, and very soon they would be able to raise their own provisions. It is specially for the information of such that these facts are now stated, for, from enquiries which have hitherto been made, it may fairly be inferred that there are thousands who would willingly come here if they thought they could secure homes and make a living for themselves and families, but who either have not known of the country, or have not known in what quarter to seek the information desired. The best months to look for land are: in the spring, May, and in the fall, August, September, or October. In these months the flies, which are troublesome mainly in June or July, are avoided; nor does the snow prevent a thorough examination of the land being made. To those without experience it has often been said that they had better obtain employment with a farmer—if possible on a new farm—for a year or so at first, so that they may have an opportunity of learning the specialties of Canadian farming. In this, however, each must judge for himself. Many would be better to do this before attempting to clear a farm for themselves. Two or three brothers may do well together, but it seems never to answer for friends to join in partnership in clearing a farm. It is often done—generally the parties are inexperienced—but the result is invariably a separation before long, and a state of accounts that is very difficult to adjust. The new settler should be careful to select his very best land for his first clearing, and to lay out his improvements systematically. It is during the first two or three years he is in most need of the best return he can get from the land, and of economizing his time, and of cultivating properly what he has in hand. These things, which seem so obvious, are more generally neglected than one would imagine, and are the greatest causes of want of success in the bush. Appended will be found a statement of the route and cost of reaching here, and a short statement of the cost of articles necessary to be purchased.

In conclusion, it has been desired to abstain from using enticing language to induce settlers to come here. There seemed to be a call for information respecting the country, and it is the humble endeavor of this pamphlet impartially to supply that want. We can only add from our experience that those who come here will find a country fit for habitation, civil, kind neighbours, and a hearty welcome.

QUERIES AND ANSWERS.

I submit the following as specimens of letters which I daily receive, together with my answers, which from their multiplicity must necessarily be brief. Thousands of anxious enquirers will gain much information by reading them:—

1. Is any portion of the Free Grant Lands tolerably free of stones and rocks?

Yes, some places entirely free, with 70 per cent. fit for cultivation.

2. What is the quality of the soil, kinds of timber growing on it, &c.?

Sandy loam; timber, mixed, a good deal of hardwood.

3. What kinds of crops are raised, and their quality?

All kinds of crops raised here, and the yield is good.

4. Are there many settlers in the District, and how do they thrive?

There are thousands of settlers, and they all thrive well and like the country.

5. Is there good employment for laborers generally?

Abundance of employment for all who are able and willing to work.

6. Is there much game there, such as deer, mink, foxes, &c.?

Plenty of game, and money to be made by hunting and trapping.

7. Are there many trappers engaged in trapping there?

There are some, but yet there is room for more; the country is large.

8. Do you think trapping and hunting would pay there for the winter?

I know some who follow it, and they succeed admirably.

Saint Pancras, Middlesex, London, England.
Guardians of the Poor, St. Pancras Workhouse, N.W.
December 26, 1870.

Sir,—Seeing your letter addressed "To the Editor of the Montreal *Daily Witness*," published in a pamphlet giving information to intending emigrants, printed at Toronto, 1869, I am induced to ask you a few questions.

First.—What is the climate of Draper? And how low does the thermometer register?

Secondly.—What is the price of good land—cleared and uncleared?

Thirdly.—The cost of living?

Fourth.—Is there any wild fowl or game to shoot?

Fifth.—Any information that you may think desirable for emigrants to know.

OFFICE OF THE "NORTHERN ADVOCATE,"
BRACEBRIDGE, 17th January, 1871.

MR. ——, London, N.W.

SIR,—Your favour of the 26th ult. received. In reply I beg to state that the climate of Draper is very healthful. We have a few cold days in winter, say one week, when the thermometer goes down, say from 20° to 30° below zero; but we are so protected by furs, &c., that we rather enjoy it, and with care no injury is done. Cleared land may be bought at from $20 to $25 dollars an acre, uncleared from $1 to $5—our dollar being equal to about four shillings sterling. The cost of living here is much cheaper than in England, as you see by enclosed list of Bracebridge markets; besides you sit free of rent, and firewood costs you nothing but the trouble of cutting it. Game is very plentiful, especially deer and partridges, while our rivers and lakes abound with the choicest fish.

I herewith send you a copy of the *Northern Advocate*, which will give you much information regarding the Free Grant Lands. I may just add, that Col. Maude, C.B., V.C., has purchased a beautiful property in Draper, and enjoys it very much.

Yours very sincerely,
THOMAS McMURRAY.

———

CHURCH STREET, TORONTO,
December 15th, 1870.

THOMAS McMURRAY, ESQ.

DEAR SIR,—Your name having been mentioned to me as a gentleman who would be able to give me some information as to the Muskoka District, I trust you will excuse the liberty I have taken in addressing you. It being my intention to settle somewhere in these parts, could you tell me the general quality of the Free Grant Lands? How far from a town or village? Whether there are good markets? The crops that could be suitably raised?

The timber on the land? Whether there are streams near? Would any be suitable for stock-raising? any easy facilities for trading? The nearest place of worship? The amount of capital that would be required to work a farm, three being in partnership? Also, are there any improved lands for sale? And any other information you can give. Also, what should you advise us to do, take Free Grants or improved land. By kindly letting us know, you will confer a great favor, and—

Yours, obediently.

————

BRACEBRIDGE, 20th Dec., 1870.

DEAR SIR, - Your favor received. The soil is generally of a sandy loam, although there is some heavy clay loam. Free Grant land can still be had within a few miles of a village. We have a good cash market for all surplus produce and stock. You can raise every kind of crop here that can be grown in the County of York. There are some ridges of pine, but the bulk of the timber is maple, basswood, elm, birch, and other descriptions of hardwood. This country abounds with living streams. There is no better country in the Dominion for stock farming than this. Cattle and sheep do well here, and pay. The facilities for travelling are good for so new a country. There are places of worship all through the districts, and schools are being everywhere organized. I cannot say how much capital it would take to work a farm, unless you state the quantity proposed to be put under cultivation. Partnerships are not desirable, in my opinion, in farming. There are improved farms for sale, prices ranging from two to ten dollars an acre. I consider it a great advantage to get a partially improved place, if you have not to pay too high for the improvements. If a man has little help, it is well to have a small clearance to begin with; but where a man has a number of strong sons, able to wield the axe, unless he can get a bargain of a place, he had better go right back into the bush, and take up a block of wild land. The *Northern Advocate* newspaper will give you much valuable information. See copy forwarded by this mail.

Yours very sincerely,

Thos. McMurray.

I have so often been asked, What can a partially cleared farm be bought for? and what capital is required to work the same? In reply to these questions, I submit the following:—

A farm containing 200 acres, with comfortable log house, barn and stable thereon, with 40 acres cleared and fenced, can be purchased for £400 or less. To work a farm of 40 acres, it would require

		£	s.	d.	
1 yoke cattle		20	0	0	stg.
	Plough	3	4	0	
	Waggon	15	0	0	
	Harrows, &c.	5	0	0	
3	Cows	16	0	0	
20	Sheep	16	0	0	
	Sow in pig	2	0	0	
	Poultry	1	10	0	
	Cost of Seed	20	0	0	
6	Months keep	50	0	0	
		148	14	0	

The returns would be

	£	s.	d.
10 acres wheat, 200 bushels, at $1	40	0	0
10 " Oats, 400 " at 50cts	40	0	0
10 " Peas, 300 " at 50cts	37	8	0
10 " Hay, potatoes and turnips	30	0	0
Profits from cows, sheep, poultry, &c	30	0	0
	177	8	0

Now, if we deduct the £70 charged for seed and keep, we have a net profit of over £100 stg. a year; so that four years would pay for the entire farm, or, if you were not prepared to purchase, and wanted to rent the cleared land, you might do so for about £20 a year.

PRICES OF NECESSARY ARTICLES.

Oxen	$100.00 to	$120.00
Cow	25.00 to	30.00
Sheep	4.00 to	6.00
Cooking Stove	20.00	
Shovel Plough	10.00	
Pork (fresh) per 100 lbs.	5.00 to	6.00
Flour, per barrel	7.00	
Harrow, Teeth, per lb.	0.10	
Axe	1.00 to	1.50
Potatoes, per bushel	0.30 to	0.50

Grindstone, from 2 to 3 cents per lb.

ROUTE FROM TORONTO TO THE MUSKOKA DISTRICT.

Toronto to Bracebridge (Summer route), distance 124 miles, fare.. $3 75

Toronto to Rosseau (Summer route), distance 140 miles, fare.. 4 15

Trains leave Toronto for Lake Simcoe steamers, and their regular through connexion, twice a day (Sundays excepted):—

For the steamer Emily May, at Bell Ewart, trains leave the city at 7 a.m.

For the steamer Ida Burton, at Barrie, trains leave the city at 4 p.m.

Toronto to Bracebridge (winter route), distance 126 miles, fare .... $4.50.

Trains leave for Barrie daily (Sundays excepted) at 7 a.m. connecting with daily stages for Muskoka, via Orillia.

INDUCEMENTS TO EMIGRATE.

Canadians may well feel proud of their country, for none under Heaven can boast of greater advantages than the inhabitants of our beloved Dominion. Peace and plenty, contentment and prosperity, characterize all the Provinces united in this grand Confederation; but the Province with which we stand more closely identified surpasses all the rest in attractiveness and good fortune.

There are many things which the people of Ontario, without any egotism, may justly boast of. Here we have all the elements essential to a nation's greatness, and a nation's wealth. The inhabitants possess intelligence and self-reliance. The soil is the richest on the continent, and our climate the healthiest in the world. Here we have a large field for all. The capitalist can find ample scope for his wealth, and the laborer abundance in employment and good remuneration for his services.

Our system of education, under the able superintendence of the Rev. E. Ryerson, LL.D., is deservedly the admiration of the world, and is now acknowledged a *model* for other nations to imitate; while our Municipal Institutions illustrate the advantages of local self-government, and are well adapted for the development of our country; in fact, so highly are they held in estimation that the Emperor of Russia recently sent Commissioners into our Province to become practically acquainted with their workings, so as to introduce them into his territory.

The scenery of Ontario is varied and grand. There is Niagara with its world-renowned cataracts, Hamilton with its mountain, and Muskoka which stands unequalled for its chain of enchanting lakes. Here we enjoy the utmost liberty, and can boast of freedom beyond even that of the mother country. Our magnificent forests are free, and you can roam where you will without running the risk of aristocratic vengeance, while our beautiful streams abounding with fish, may, in their season, be enjoyed by all without molestation. I believe in the sentiment, "that all men are born free and equal." Here men are measured, not by their gold, nor the extent of their domains, but by their moral worth. Hence all stand upon a grand equality, so that the honest poor man is as much respected as the millionaire. Another thing that marks the progress of civilization, and which we may well rejoice at, is the deep, practical sympathy manifested for a class who have strong claims upon our benevolence; and if it be the duty of the Government to provide for those who are deprived of their senses that duty has been nobly discharged by the present ministry, for in two years they have given somewhere about $600,000 to charitable and benevolent objects, and certainly the blessing of the blind, as well as that of the deaf and dumb will rest upon them. They have also inaugurated a system, with reference to the treatment of the insane, that will immortalize their administration. Mr. Langmuir, inspector of prisons, informed us that some 300 lunatics have been taken from the jails and placed under favorable treatment, whereby twenty-five per cent. have been cured; and, of all the cases brought under their notice within the last two years, no fewer than 57 per cent. have been discharged cured.

A great saving has been effected in this department as well. Hitherto all lunatics were confined, and not only was this confinement detrimental to their recovery, but it was a source of great expense to the country. Now, however, only dangerous lunatics are kept in this way, and harmless ones are permitted to move about and make themselves useful, and thereby a great saving is gained.

It is gratifying to know that Canada which takes the lead in educational matters is also leading the way in other charitable ways, and the present Administration deserve no small credit for what they have done in the various reforms, which characterize their administration; but still we venture to assert that the crowning glory of their administration will ultimately be found in what they have done, and will yet do to open up this new country, and fill the Free Grant Districts with countless thousands of loyal settlers who will make Muskoka second to no part of Canada in wealth and importance.

For the encouragement of those about to emigrate, and as a proof of our prosperity, we give the following from the Ottawa *Times*:—

"We understand that the Customs and Internal revenue receipts for the months of July and August show an increase of considerable more than half a million dollars over the corresponding period of last year. Only about $150,000 of this is consequent upon changes in tariff; the balance is entirely the result of largely increased amount of business done in the country. What makes it the more gratifying is the fact that the increase is general throughout the Dominion, not being confined to one or two cities, and thus indicating a condition of general prosperity, which is in the highest degree satisfactory."

Here wages are higher, and food is cheaper than in England, while our taxation is a mere nothing. Nor is there the slightest probability that the labour market will be glutted, for of all the thousands of emigrants who arrived last year, the demand continues, while wages remain as high as before.

Canada, therefore, offers a home where all the necessaries of life can be enjoyed by those who are able and willing to work, with perfect security to life and property.

It should then be the object of every lover of his country, of every one who believes in British institutions, and desires that the largest possible number of his fellow-subjects should share in the benefits the nearest, greatest and cheapest of British colonial dependencies has to bestow, to set forth her claims to their first choice, and thus prevent many thousands who cross the Atlantic from becoming alienated from their allegiance to their motherland.

The *Globe* of December 28th, 1870, says:—"The perfectly free and liberal character of our political constitution, the complete control the people can, if they will, exercise in their Federal, Provincial and Municipal government, should remove all difficulty out of the way of the latter half of our proposition. As to the former—so far as countries speaking the English tongue are concerned—it would seem that the desirable point has been already attained. With respect to the prime necessaries of life, Canada may certainly compare very favourably with any British colony, and they are to be had far cheaper here than in Great Britain or the United States.

"With respect to taxation, however, the advantages are in favour of Canada beyond all comparison. The taxation per head in the Dominion is only 18s. 11d. sterling. In Great Britain and Ireland it is £2 4s. 7d., or about two and a half times the amount of our proportion. In the United States it is £2 19s. 5d. per head, or more than three times that of Canada. But the taxation of the other British Colonies places that of Canada in a still more favourable light. In New Zealand the taxation is actually £12 7s. 2d. per head; in South Australia, £6 7s. 4d. per head; in Queensland, £5 13s. 9d. per head; and in New South Wales, £5 6s. 9d. per head. Thus Canada is taxed only in the proportion, in round figures, of one-thirteenth of New Zealand—less than one-sixth of South Australia—one-sixth of Queensland—and something over one-fifth of New South Wales.

"At the present moment there can be no doubt that thousands of persons in Great Britain are contemplating emigration during the coming summer. The industrious millions of the old country can find an outlet for their over-stocked labour market, where wages—we speak, of course, of handicrafts and agricultural employment—are higher than at home, where food is cheaper and where the hand of the tax-gatherer is most lightly felt. Nor is there the least fear of the supply of hands exceeding the means of employment."

FREE GRANTS OF LAND.

Heads of families get a grant of 200 acres of land, and each member of his family, over 18 years of age, 100 acres; and, if more is wanted, each settler can purchase 100 acres, at 50 cents an acre, cash. The conditions are residence on the lot at least six months a year. There shall be cleared during each year not less than 2 acres. At the end of five years, the deed will be issued. A Homestead law provides that, if the first settler or his heirs remain on the land, it cannot be seized for debt for 20 years. This Free Grant system has already proved a great stimulus to the settlement of country, and I look for yet greater results.

THE SETTLERS.

A better class of people never took possession of a new settlement than the inhabitants of these Districts. Here you will find all classes, rich and poor, learned and unlearned, fired with the same zeal and working for the same object, namely, to prepare an independent home and improve their circumstances. Already we have some thousands of settlers, the greater part belonging to the sons of toil, and they are daily on the increase. The nationality, as far as we can judge, is as follows: one-third Canadian, one-third Protestant Irish, one-third composed of English, Scotch and German.

Great credit is due to the first settlers; they had to endure many hardships and privations. Lumberers and steamboat owners have certainly done much for the country, but the early pioneers deserve the medal.

I have spent hours listening with the deepest attention to those aged heroes as they related the thrilling incidents connected with their early history. There is a wonderful pleasure in the realization of the fact, that, after years of weary toil, a competency has been acquired and a comfortable home provided. We have seen a man stand in front of his mansion, gazing upon a country that was cleared for miles, and heard him exclaim, with pride, "When I came to these parts, there was not a tree cut nor a settler within twenty miles of me." What a change has taken place! The woodsman's axe has been at work, and now you gaze upon a landscape of surpassing beauty. Numerous farm houses appear in view, giving evidence of comfort and prosperity; herds of cattle are grazing upon the pasture lands, orchards are laden with the choicest fruits, and fields of golden grain are waving in the breeze, where, a few years ago, the foot of white man never trod. Monuments have been raised to men less worthy than some of those pioneers who have done so much to raise Canada to the position which it now occupies among the nations of the earth. But, for the early pioneers, no marble monument is erected:

> They sleep is secret, and their sod
> Unknown to man, is marked by God.

Settlement in 1871 is easy work compared with what it was in the early history of the Province. Now we have the Colonization Roads running through the very centre of our Free Grant territory, so that settlers can easily, cheaply and quickly make their way to their new homes; whereas the early settlers had no such advantages. Many of them had to ford streams and follow Indian trails for miles to reach their locations; some had to go from 40 to 50 miles for their seed and pack it home upon their backs all that distance. Then it was no rare thing to have to go 40 miles with a bushel of wheat to the mill and take the flour home again. Some who are living to-day in splendid houses, and who own magnificent farms, have gone over 40 miles for their first bushel of seed potatoes.

THE BACKWOODSMAN'S SONG.

NOTE.—I give this, not because of any merit which it possesses, but from the fact that it was the first piece of poetry published on Muskoka, and was written by one of the oldest settlers.

TUNE—*Auld Lang Syne.*

Come to the land of rivers,
    And groves of goodly pine—
A land to last forever,
    To be both yours and mine;
Our rulers now, God bless them,
    In wisdom they designed
Free grants of land to give away
    In this most favored clime.

One hundred acres every man
    Shall have on terms good
Only to come and lead the van
    To grand Muskoka's wood.
Here are the falls of splendour,
    Magnificent and grand;
And here are nature's wonders
    On these free tracts of land.

Here may the angler's wishes
    Be more than satisfied;
A good shot may make riches
    Down by the Severn side.
The Severn in his grandeur,
    Which dashes from rock to rock,
Reminds us of our native land,
    Our fathers and their flock.

Then come along, young men of sense,
    Bring axes and bring hoes;
Begin your farms now to clear—
    The woods resound with blows.
Your old friends and your comrades

May wish to live at ease;
Take courage, boys, and come along,
It will your sweethearts please.

The townships are laid out in lots,
The road on either side,
From Severn to Muskoka Falls,
Is ample, good and wide.
On either side you may now have
Those lands, as not located;
But if you do not come in time
You're sure to be defeated.

Then here's a cheer for our good Queen,
For Britons we are still;
We have the hearts to fell the woods,
And work with a good will.
Our homes shall be in these wild woods,
Our daughters, young and fair,
Will sing around our bright log fires,
In health, and free from care.
—W. MERCIER.

There is nothing like taking up land in a new and prosperous settlement, and there is no way that a man will accumulate more money than by adopting this course, as the history of thousands can testify, as every year your property is increasing in value. I could enumerate many instances of men who came to Canada without a shilling in their pockets, who, by taking up land in a new settlement when it was cheap, grew up with the place, and amassed great wealth.

The Oshawa *Vindicator* says that Dr. McGill and Mr. Glen have sold to Mr. Thomas Conlin 100 acres of timber land for $8,500. This makes Mr. Conlin the owner of 700 acres of land, all within the township of East Whitby. Mr. Conlin came to this country with only one shilling in his pocket, and by great industry, good judgement and prudence, he has become one of the largest land-owners in the township. This is the kind of men to build up a country, and this is the country for that kind of men.

Tenant farmers and others who would sell out, and realize say from £200 and upwards, could do well here; for while it costs $20 an acre (equal to about £4 stg.) to clear the land, the first crop generally pays for that, and hence it proves a good investment.

THE ADVANTAGES OF MUSKOKA.

These are both varied and substantial. It is within easy access of Toronto, and is on the direct line of the Overland Route to the great North-West. It is also as I have shown in a previous chapter, almost on a bee line of travel on the shortest route from the Atlantic to the Pacific; besides, it is likely to be penetrated by the Sault Ste. Marie and Ottawa River Railway, and now the certainty of the construction of the Toronto, Simcoe and Muskoka Junction Railway to the village of Bracebridge is a fixed fact. While, at the same time, it possesses a very large extent of country, 70 per cent. of which is fit for cultivation, and its water facilities are unsurpassed on the American continent. The importance of the water-power which this country contains cannot be over-estimated. It is designed to be an important manufacturing country, and may one day be the very workshop of Canada itself. As a stock-raising country it will stand unrivalled in the Province; besides, minerals have been found in sufficient quantities to satisfy even the most incredulous, that this whole section abounds with the riches treasures which will be developed at no very distant date. As for stock farming, Muskoka will be to Ontario what the Highlands of Scotland is to the Lowlands of Scotland. It will be a great nursery for sheep and cattle; the land is both high and rolling; it is well watered, and a very rich grazing country, and when it becomes linked by the Railway to Toronto the market will be very little inferior to that great centre. Then there is considerable timber, both pine and hemlock, and, as it is now demonstrated that the latter contains an extract which is very valuable, it must prove an increasing source of wealth. Competent judges say that it is worth 20 per cent. more than pine timber.

It is now generally admitted that Muskoka possesses many advantages, and that it has made rapid progress.

THE FIRST NEWSPAPER.

The first newspaper in the Settlement was published by the author, on the 14th day of September, 1869, bearing the title of the *"Northern Advocate."* It was first printed at Parry Sound, but from the fact that Bracebridge was more central it has been removed thither. The object of the publisher was to give reliable information about the Free Grant Lands, and his labours have been very successful. The circulation is 1,000 copies weekly. A great many copies go to England, Ireland and Scotland for the information of intending emigrants, and through its advocacy many have been induced to settle in our midst.

It is somewhat singular, that when the writer first came to Muskoka, he had to row across Muskoka lake, and when the first issue of the *Northern Advocate* was published, it so happened that the steamer was under repairs, and he had to row 16 miles across the same water in order to deliver the first number.

We have a most flourishing Agricultural Society, the By-laws and Rules of which together with the Annual Report I respectfully submit.

By-Laws and Rules of the Muskoka Union Agricultural Society, as adopted at a Meeting of the Directors held on the 15th of February, 1870.

1st.—That this Society shall be known as the Muskoka Union Agricultural Society (which shall comprise the several Townships in the District).

2nd.—That a general public meeting shall be held in the second week of January in each year, on such day and in said week as the President shall, by notification in writing to the Secretary, given one month beforehand, appoint.

3rd.—That this Society shall be governed by a President, Vice-President, Secretary, Treasurer, and nine other Directors.

4th.—That all subscriptions shall be paid before the first day of May in each year, in default of which the member shall forfeit forthwith all benefit of membership in the current year.

5th.—Competition for prizes and all other benefits of membership shall be limited to members and to residents in the district who may, before 10 o'clock on the morning of the Show, pay double subscription, which shall entitle them to the rights of membership for the current year.

6th.—Stud Horses not to compete with Farm or Team Horses.

7th.—That a subscription of $1.00 shall entitle a member to compete for four prizes, and the payment of 12½ cents entrance fee for each entry above that number.

8th.—Stock and produce entered for exhibition must be the bona fide property of the exhibitor.

9th.—The exact age of all animals competing for prizes, being under one year old, shall be specified to the Secretary at the time of entering, and taken into consideration by the Judges.

10th.—In the absence of competition in any of the classes, the Judges will exercise their discretion in awarding a premium.

11th.—No animal to compete in any shape for more than one prize.

12th.—No farm produce of the same kind to be entered for more than one prize, but entries of different varieties of the same kind of grain will be allowed, and must be the growth or production of the year in which the exhibition is held, and from the exhibitor's own or rented estate.

13th.—All entries for the Show shall be made three days previous to the Show, or up to 10 o'clock on the morning of the Show on payment of 12½ cents to the Secretary.

14th.—The election of Judges shall be made by the Directors. No person shall be both Judge and candidate for the same prize.

15th.—That the rights of membership shall be restricted to bona fide settlers in the District of Muskoka.

16th.—That ewes must have suckled their lambs till the first day of July, and all sheep must have been regularly shorn after the 15th day of May.

17th.—That the Prize List be published at least three months before the day of Show.

From the "Northern Advocate" of 7th October, 1870.

AGRICULTURAL SHOW.

The third annual Show of the Muskoka Union of Townships Agricultural Society was held at Bracebridge on the 27th ult. The weather was most favourable. The attendance large and respectable, and the whole proceedings proved a great success.

We were very much impressed with the vast progress that has been made during the past year. The quantity and quality of the stock and produce exhibited, astonished all present. The cattle shown called forth the admiration of visitors. Some competent judges said that the oxen were equal to any that they had ever seen at the Provincial Fair.

The display of produce was very large, and the samples would compare favourably with any county in Ontario.

The show of vegetables and roots was large, and very complete. The tomatoes, melons, pumpkins, squash, cauliflowers, beets, potatoes, etc., were equal to anything that we ever saw, and went far to dispel the delusion of those who imagine that we cannot raise those things to advantage. In the Free Grant Districts the dairy produce exhibited is worthy of much commendation, and fully justifies what we have for years advocated, that this country is admirably adapted for stock-raising and diary purposes.

The ladies' department was very attractive, and reflected

great credit upon the good taste and ability of the Muskoka ladies. Some of the articles shown displayed great ingenuity, and wonderful perseverance. Truly they are ministering angels and "patterns of patience."

The contrast between the Show of 1870 and that of last year is very much striking, and speaks well for the prosperity of the District. In 1869 only one sample of butter was exhibited; this year we had 24. In 1869 no bread was shown; in 1870 we had 12 samples. In 1869 only one piece of ladies' work was entered; in 1870 over 50 vied with each other, and so all through the different departments. A decided improvement was noticeable, and next year we anticipate even greater success.

The annual dinner of the Society was held at the "Dominion House," and was got up in splendid style by Mr. B.W. Ross.

The chair was occupied by John Teviotdale, Esq., President of the Society, Reeve of Draper, etc.; the vice-chair by A.H. Browning, Esq., Reeve of Monck. After the cloth was removed, the President rose and proposed "The Queen" and other loyal toasts, which were well received. The toast, "The Army and Navy" was ably responded to by ex-Captain Slaven, of Orillia, who, in a graphic speech, alluded to the time when the soil of our frontier was polluted by a band of Fenian invaders; and when duty called him to go to defend our homes, and signified his willingness on a moment's notice to do so again. He considered that Canada would be in a position at no very distant date to boast of a military force equal to any in the world. He paid a high tribute to the soldier-like qualities of the Volunteers of Canada, and predicted that, if properly officered, they would yet distinguish themselves, and prove to the world that they were neither lacking in skill nor courage.

"The Red, White and Blue" was then sung by Mr. Rich. James Bell.

In reply to the toast, "Our Local Members," John Morrison, Esq., M.P., said that he felt very thankful for the cordial reception he had met with, and the enthusiastic manner in which the company had received the toast. He felt that it was his duty to apologize to the settlers for not visiting Muskoka before this; but he promised that whether he should seek to represent North Victoria again or no, he would, if spared, return to this section. He spoke of the scenery as being most romantic and picturesque, and said it reminded him of the Highlands of Scotland. He expressed himself much surprised at the amount of land that he had seen fit for agricultural purposes. He had no idea until his arrival, that Muskoka was as good a country as it is; but what surprised him most, was the number and respectable appearance of the settlers. He considered that a railroad would prove a great benefit to the settlement, and thought that the Government could not do better than apply some of their large surplus to assist in the construction of the Muskoka Junction Railway. Thanking the rate-payers for the liberal support given him at the last election, and promising to return again at no very distant date, he took his seat amidst loud applause.

A.P. Cockburn, Esq., M.P.P. said that he felt in duty bound to return his sincere thanks to the gentlemen present for the hearty manner in which the toast had been received. It was to him a source of pleasure and of pride to be surrounded by so many warm friends. He was perfectly delighted with the whole proceedings of the day, and the success which attended the Muskoka Union of Townships Agricultural Society was far beyond his most sanguine expectations. He considered that the show which they had witnessed to-day, would go far to elevate the district in the estimation of those who had come from a distance, as they had evidence before them in the products of the country which had been exposed, that must satisfy every candid person. He alluded to the spirit of enterprise which was everywhere manifested, and predicted a great future for this country. He thought that a railroad was just what was wanted to settle up this north country, and was of opinion that every member of the house would go in favour of giving a grant to the Toronto, Simcoe and Muskoka Junction Railway, as soon as it touched Free Grant Territory. He promised to watch over the interests of the settlement, and do all in his power to promote its interests.

"The Judges" were next toasted. Mr. Arch. Thompson, in replying, said that he was much pleased with the Show, and considered that the stock exhibited would compete with any north of Toronto.

Mr. J. Cuppage admitted that he came with his mind prejudiced against Muskoka, but he confessed that "a change came over the spirit of his dream," and he was about to leave with very favorable impressions of the country. He had often witnessed worse oxen at the Provincial Fair than had been exhibited today, and wished us increasing success.

Mr. Peter Nisbet, (Pickering Township) was surprised at the quality of the road leading into the district, and at the active signs of life which were seen in Bracebridge. He had been examining men and things since his arrival, and was forcibly struck with the very intelligent, and highly respectable appearance of the inhabitants. He expressed himself pleased with the show, and said that the dairy department was superior, that the fowl shown were choice, and the cattle numerous and excellent in quality. He was about to leave the settlement with a good impression, not only of the country but also of the people.

Mr. Taylor was glad that the strangers were disappointed "agreeably, and that they found the show better than they had anticipated. He also made a vigorous speech, setting forth the progress of the Society.

Mr. W. Sharpe said that when he was locating here, some of his friends were afraid that he would not be able to live in Muskoka; but he was glad to state after an experience of six years that he found that he could not only live by farming in Muskoka, but he was able to do more.

"The Agricultural interests of the District" was replied to by

Mr. Paul Dane, who evidently is not very friendly to the "powers that be." His speech was noted for its originality, and caused considerable merriment.

Mr. Albert Spring strongly defended the Government, and stated that he did not expect them to build a road to his door. He thought that if the Government made the great leading highway into the settlement, that that was all that could reasonably be expected from them, and the settlers should make roads connecting with the colonization roads. He held that the Government had done a great deal for Muskoka, and that they deserved the hearty thanks of every settler in the district. He claimed to be a railroad man, and considered that all we wanted here in order to make a first rate country was a railroad. He was convinced that this district would be a great stock-producing section, and we required the "iron horse" to bring us into contact with Toronto, where we could find a ready sale for fat cattle. He thought that the Government could not better promote the interests of immigration than by giving a liberal grant towards the building of the Muskoka Junction Railway. He was a poor man; but, knowing the advantages of railroad communication, he would willingly subscribe $200 to assist the enterprise; and, considering the expense of bringing in goods under the present arrangement, it would be to our advantage to give a liberal bonus, and by so doing we would be gainers.

"Our Guests" was next proposed, and heartily responded to, after which Dr. Gunn (Whitby) remarked that he could not but admire the road; although he had to confess that on entering the settlement he was very much discouraged at the appearance of so much rock; but, as he neared the Fort of Gibraltar, and saw the flag waving in the breeze, he thought that there must after all be a country beyond worth defending, and he had found it really so. There was a prevailing opinion outside that Muskoka was unfit for settlement, but this was attributable to ignorance. He spoke of the grandeur of the scenery, and the healthfulness of the climate, and said that even Saratoga was not to be compared to it. His party had greatly enjoyed their trip. They had found that the sail had given an increase to their spirits, vigor and appetite. He paid a high compliment to A.P. Cockburn, Esq., M.P.P., and the officers on board the "Wenonah" for the excellent accommodation furnished, and the courteous attention paid to visitors while sailing on that comfortable steamer. He designated Muskoka a great safety valve, where enterprising Canadians might come and find scope for the development of all their energies. He spoke highly of the intelligence of the settlers, commended their appreciation of education, and complimented them upon the strict observance of the Sabbath which he had observed throughout the settlement. He thought that Muskoka was well adapted for butter and cheese-making, and concluded by wishing the district continued success.

The Rev. Alex. Kennedy (Pickering) remarked that he was of opinion that this district would at no distant date form a very important part of the Dominion of Canada. The right men were in the right place. They possessed all the elements necessary to bring this about; for he could see that the settlers were men who possessed self-reliance, and were not easily discouraged; and, if they continued as they had commenced, they would yet see such prosperity as would make them glad. He, with the other speakers, was favorably impressed with both the country and the people.

J.B. Browning, Esq., rose and said that he was delighted to meet with his old friends once more. At the commencement of the Society's operations, he acted as Secretary, and took deep interest in its welfare, and now he felt rejoiced at the measure of success which had followed the efforts put forth. He said it was a law in nature to know no vacuum; so, although he was called away to another sphere of action, his place had at once been supplied by a gentleman who had nobly discharged the onerous duties of Secretary, and he would not detain them with a speech, but simply propose the health of Rich. Jas. Bell, Esq., the Secretary of the M.U. of Townships Agricultural Society.

Mr. Bell, in reply, returned his hearty and sincere thanks to the gentlemen present for the enthusiastic manner in which the toast had been received, and said that the noble day which they were so pleasantly bringing to a close caused his heart to swell with pleasure.

"The Press" was ably replied to by Mr. John C. McMullen (Orillia), who claimed to be the pioneer pressman of the district. Having many years ago written several articles in defence of the country,

"The Health of the Ladies" was responded to by Mr. J.B. Browning and Mr. John McAree.

"The Health of the President, Vice-President, and Officers of the Society" was next proposed and responded to by John Teviotdale, Esq., and A.H. Browning, Esq.

"The Lumbering interests" was replied to by H.H. Cook, Esq., who claimed to be one of the pioneers of Muskoka,—having travelled through it for the past 14 years getting out square timber. He described his limits as covering 300 square miles, and said that the settlers got about ten times as much for their square timber as for saw logs. He considered the Show a great success, and pronounced it one of the best he ever attended. He alluded to the enterprise and perseverance of Mr. A.P. Cockburn, M.P.P., in putting the "Wenonah" upon Lake Muskoka at so early a period in the history of the settlement; and, thanking the President for the honor conferred upon him, was followed by J.D. Macaulay, Esq., local agent for the extensive firm of Messrs. Dodge & Co., who claimed that lumbering was a great blessing to the settlers. It put money in circulation, gave employment during the winter months, furnished a cash market for all surplus produce, and prepared the way for railroad facilities. He was satisfied this would be a well-settled and prosperous part of Canada before long, and complimented the settlers on their intelligence and courtesy.

"The Mechanical interests of Bracebridge" was replied to by Mr. D.H. Cameron and Mr. Robert Ferguson. The former thought that the Society should in future award prizes to manufacturers as well as to farmers, that the success of a country depended as much upon the one as the other.

The latter thought that Muskoka was second to no place in Canada for hospitality and kindness to strangers. Here we knew how to entertain strangers. He did not regret leaving the city of Toronto to carve out a home in the wilderness, for here he had pure air, sound health, and good appetite, and the prospect of a comfortable and independent home. He advised the farmers and mechanics to pull together, and stand united, and very soon Muskoka would be raised to take a prominent position among the first counties of Ontario.

"Our Host and Hostess" was replied to in a good-natured speech from Mr. B.W. Ross, the spirited proprietor.

Auld Lang Syne was then sung, and three cheers having been given to the Queen, the company separated, much pleased with the enjoyable evening they had spent.

The following is the list of prizes awarded at the third annual show of the Muskoka Union of Townships Agricultural Society, held at Bracebridge, 27th September, 1870.

HORSES.

Best Brood Mare, with foal at foot—John Teviotdale, Esq.	$ 4 00
Best Span of Horses—M. McCarthy	4 00
Second best do.—W. Sharpe	2 00

SHEEP.

Best aged Ram—Messrs. Browning	3 50
Second best—S. Willis	2 50

Best Ram Lamb—W. Tait 3 00
Second best do.—A.J. Alport, Esq 2 00
Best pen 2 Ewes—Messrs. Browning 3 00
Second best do.—W. Holditch 2 00
Best pen 2 Ewes (having raised lambs this season),—Messrs.
  Browning 3 00
Second best do.—W. Tait 2 00
Best 2 Ewe Lambs—W. Holditch 2 50
Second best do.—Alexander Barron 1 50

SWINE.

Best Boar, over nine months old,—Thomas George 3 00
Best breeding Sow—T. George 3 00
Second best do.—W. Sharpe 2 00

CATTLE.

Best Bull—Thomas Keal, jun. 5 00
Second best do.—G. Scholey, sen. 3 00
Best Bull Calf—J. Teviotdale, Esq. 2 00
Best Milch Cow—   do.   do. 4 00
Second best do.—W. Sharpe 2 00
Best yearling Heifer—W. Sharpe 2 00
Second best do.—W. Ennis 1 00
Best 2 year old Heifer—W. Sharpe 2 00
Second best do.—M. Moore 1 00
Best Heifer Calf—A. Black 2 00
Best Yoke Working Oxen—James Prunty 4 00
Second best do.—P. Managan 2 50
Best Yoke 3 year old Steers—W. Ennis 3 00
Second best do.—Charles Edgar 2 00

POULTRY.

Best Goose and Gander—J. Tookey 0 75
Second best do.—W. Sharpe 0 50

Best Turkey and Gobbler—John Teviotdale, Esq.	0 75
Best Rooster and 2 Hens—John Teviotdale, Esq.	0 75
Second best do.—James Tookey	0 50
Best Duck and Drake—John Teviotdale, Esq.	0 75
Second best do.— do. do.	0 50

PRODUCE.

Best two bushels Fall Wheat—A.J. Alport, Esq.	3 00
Best two bushels Spring Wheat—W. Tait	3 00
Second best do—Messrs. Browning	2 00
Best two bushels Oats—John Teviotdale, Esq.	2 00
Second best do—A.J. Alport, Esq.	1 50
Best two bushels Peas—John Teviotdale, Esq.	2 00
Best two bushels Barley—R. Ennis	2 00
Best two bushels Rye—W. Tait	2 00
Best bag Cup Potatoes—Sames Tookey	1 50
Best bag Potatoes (any kidd)—George Scholey, sen.	1 50
Best firkin Butter (10 lbs.)—Patrick Managan	3 00
Second best do—W. Tait	2 00
Best roll Fresh Butter (2 lbs.)—W. Sharpe	3 00
Second best do—J. Tookey	1 50
Best loaf home-made Bread—Nehemiah Mathews	1 50
Second best do—C. Jenkins	1 00
Best collection of garden Vegetables—Ralph Nicholson	2 00
Second best do—Charles Bard	1 50
Third best do—James Tookey	1 00

LADIES' DEPARTMENT.

Best fancy Needlework in Berlin wool—Mrs. Fenson	0 75
Best specimen Knitting—Mrs. W. Ennis	0 75
Best Patch Quilt—Mrs. R. Stewart	2 00
Second best do—Mrs. Fenson	1 00
Best 2 lbs Worsted Yarn, spun at home—Mrs. Hannah	2 00
Second best do—Mrs. J. Whitfield	1 00

EXTRA PRIZES (COMMENDED).

Span of horses, Richard Chapman; two ewe lambs, John Kelly; bull, Charles Robertson; milch cow, Messrs. Browning; heifer calf, Messrs. Browning; working oxen, Charles Jenkins, James Tookey, Messrs. Browning, Charles Bard and W. Whitfield; boots and shoes, W. Kennedy; horse shoes, Duncan Cameron; card basket, Mrs. Thomas Myers; braiding, Mrs. Thomas Myers; sample needlework, &c., Mrs. W. Kennedy; sofa pillow, Mrs. Thomas Myers; baby's jacket, &c., Mrs. Fenson; fancy needlework, Mrs. A. Barron.

TRADE.

The following is from the *Northern Advocate* of the 25th of November, 1870:—

"It is very gratifying for us to be in a position to state that the *fall trade* has been brisk, even beyond our expectations. The quantity of goods imported into the district this season is almost incredible. Still, the demand has been equal to the supply; and if large cash purchases by the settlers be any criterion of prosperity, then Muskoka is eminently prosperous—in fact, so rapidly is business increasing that a railway becomes a necessity; for although there are hundreds of teams employed in the carrying trade, they are altogether inadequate to the growing requirements of the place. Outsiders may wonder how it is that money is so plentiful in Muskoka, and that purchasing for *cash* is the *rule*, not the exception, all through the settlement. For their information, we may just state that the crops this year were abundant, and the prices realized remunerative, so that the settlers have the means within themselves to procure everything they require.

Some of our correspondence seem wonderfully anxious about a market. Their constant inquiry is, where can you find a market for your surplus grain, etc.? Why, we have it here, right at our very door. Our storekeepers will take in trade, or pay cash for any quantity of produce or raw furs; and our cattle merchants will pay cash for any number of *fat cattle*. But some may say, how long will this last? Well, we believe it will continue for years, for new settlers are pouring in so rapidly that a large quantity will be wanted to furnish them with seed, and sustain them until they raise something for themselves. Then we have extensive lumbering operations going on, thus affording employment to many, and furnishing a cash market at the same time. Few can estimate the extensive importance of the lumbering operations carried on in these parts. Here we have at work five of the largest and wealthiest lumbering firms on the *American Continent*—Messrs. Dodge & Co., Messrs. Clarke, White & Co., Messrs. Hotchkiss, Hughson & Co., Messrs. Cook Brothers, and the Bell Ewart Company. The first-named concern employs 800 men, and the others in like proportion. Who, then, can estimate the benefits derived by the united operations of those gigantic establishments? Another source of wealth to the settlers is the income derived from the sale of their saw-logs. Those who have obtained their patents realize the *entire proceeds* of their logs, and thus they are enabled to make greater improvements; hence the wonderful rapidity of the growth and development of Muskoka. But some one asks, "What will become of you when lumbering ceases?" Why settlers will then be able to "paddle their own canoe!" Already they hear the snorting of the "iron horse;" and before the home market becomes glutted, they will be in direct communications with the city of Toronto, the best market in Ontario.

SOURCES OF ENJOYMENT.

Some imagine that because we live back in the woods, we must be extremely lonely, and destitute of all means of enjoyment. This is a great mistake. We would not exchange positions with our city friends. There is no end to our sources of pleasure. If hunting is our ambition, we have any amount of sport. If fast driving is our choice, the good sleighing which we have facilitates that means of enjoyment; or, if we are fond of social gatherings, there are frequent opportunities of gratifying it to the utmost, as the following cases will illustrate:

THE SLEIGH RIDE.

Calm is the night, and clear and bright;
    The silver moon is shedding
A flood of light o'er the snow so white,
    And an icy glory spreading.
The earth looks fair as a dream of love,
    In misty light the moon does lend her,
And the starry vault of blue above
    Is sparkling bright with a frosty splendour.

Swiftly we bound o'er the frozen ground,
    Gaily, joyously, cheerily;
And our thoughts keep time to the musical chime
    Of the sleigh-bells tinkling merrily.
For our hearts are attuned to the pleasing strains
    Of gladness, glee and innocent mirth;
And we feel, tho' sin has made dark stains,
    Yet happiness lingers still on earth.

In wrap and rug, right warm and snug,
    All care to the winds we fling;
And laugh and song, as we speed along,
    Make the silent forest ring.
The distant owl our voices hears,
    And screams from his dark and lonely dell,
In answer to our joyous cheers,
    A discordant, wild, unearthly yell.

Faster we go—the frozen snow
    From our horses' feet is flying;
The echoes long repeat our song,
    Far in the distance dying.
Our joyous breasts exulting bound,

And utterance find in gleeful voice,
Till rocks, and hills, and dales resound,
And even the gloomy woods rejoice.

Our sleigh now glides where the river hides
    Under the icebridge strong,
Where deep and low the waters flow
    So silently along.
And now it is past, and on we roam,
    By the frozen lake—a snowy plain,—
Past the gleaming lights of the settler's home,
    And away through the lonely wood again.

The Falls! it is they! We can see the spray
    That the seething waters toss,
Like a glittering cloud, o'er that foaming flood;
    And now, as the bridge we cross,
Its echoing thunders louder grow.
    Check'd is our noisy mirth and song,
And we stop and gaze where far below
    The rolling torrent roars along.

The trees that stand on either hand
    Are hung with icedrops fair—
With gems of light and jewels bright,
    And dazzling crystals rare;—
Reflecting back each twinkling star,
    With a sparkling beauty rich and grand,—
A glittering scene, surpassing far
    Our wildest dreams of fairy land.

When swiftly past, in the roaring blast,
    The frost king sweeps in his pride,
His icy form the raging storm
    And the mantling snow wreath hide.
And unseen spirits the way prepare,
    Wherever his royal feet would go,
With dazzling carpets, white and fair,
    And the crystal bridge where waters flow.

I love the clink, on the frozen rink,
  Of the skater's iron heel;
The merry huzza of the boys at play
  With their sleds, on the slippery hill;
The long, long nights, by the bright fire-side,
  In the joyous home where happiness dwells;
And best of all, the merry sleigh-ride,
  And the musical chime of the tinkling bells.

WOOL PICKING BEE.

Sir,—Understanding one of the objects of your columns being to convey abroad information concerning our great country, as well as to supply means of edification to our own people—the settlers. It may, I think, be fairly regarded as a needful part of your work to give the outsiders some idea of bush life, as well as land. One of the questions, no doubt, arising in the minds of those moving in, would very likely be: How do the poor folks make out to pass their evenings? or, have they anything corresponding to missionary breakfasts, complimentary dinners, or oyster suppers? Some sketches of real life in the bush might serve the purpose of answering such questions. A "wool picking bee" (let me guard against being misunderstood), does not mean an insect of the bee kind peculiar to this region, and noted for picking the wool of the sheep, but is the name for a kind of affair which will be best understood by a brief description of a sing "bee." The one I had the privilege of attending was got up by a lady inviting her friends and neighbours on a given evening. A goodly number accepting, they assembled and commenced operations around a large home-made table, by teasing the tufts of wool, preparatory to further manufacture; meanwhile some of the young people were good naturedly teasing one another. Amongst the company present might be noticed the various functionaries of the locality, as trappers, postmaster, preachers, pathmasters, school teachers, miscellaneous traders, etc., and in most cases several offices meeting in the same individual, and all claiming the addition B.W. (i.e., bush whacker), and not least, the correspondent of the *Northern Advocate*. But now the work and amusement proceed in unison, which is more than can always be accomplished. Interspersed, moreover, with something of edification, and not altogether without a religious bearing, hymn singing, and a trifle of political and theological discussion, etc.

> Here in bush life is found,
> Work and play both abound,
> And yet strangely agree;
> Here extremes we'd unite,
> Here the sombre and bright,
> Mixed together you see;
> Unrestrained seem to run
> Both the serious and fun
> In the "Wool-Picking Bee."

About noon of night, there might, perhaps, be noticed a shade of falling off in the spirit of wool-picking, when a sound is heard indicating a change of scene and a variety in the exercises to be introduced, of which one might for an hour or two previously have smelled the approach. Preparations are ordered, the wool is speedily removed, and picking of another kind introduced. It might do in the city to say "the delicacies of the season;" but here the dishes, or what was on them, would require somewhat varied terms to describe. It was in fact a great meal, of which the items would be more tedious to describe than they were to discuss practically. A roast beaver might, perhaps, be the most notable deviation from ordinary fare, but breakfast, dinner, and supper were so amply represented, that a good old-style brother declared the big table to be wickedly piled luxuries, when a youngster replied: "If this be wickedness I hope to be always a sinner." It is not too much to say that *full* justice was done in relieving the rude table from its cause of groaning; so, having picked the wool, the bones of the beaver, and chickens, and singing the doxology, each seemed disposed to pick a partner, and the "bee" stood adjourned *sine die*. This I must say in conclusion, for the relief of some of your uninitiated readers who may feel a kind of commiseration for the sadness of poor bush life, and would start with alarm to hear of a wool picking bee; had they only the chance of taking part in the affair they might be more disposed to envy than pity; and I seriously advise them, if ever they get an invitation to a wool-picking bee, go.

Draper, October 26, 1869.

The *Northern Advocate* of the 27th January, 1871, contains the following:—

CHURCH OF ENGLAND CONCERT.

The concert held on Friday evening was a grand success, reflecting much credit upon those who made the arrangements, and deserved praise to the ladies and gentlemen who carried out so efficiently the excellent programme.

We regret that want of space prevents us from entering into full particulars; but still it affords us much pleasure to state, that the Hall was brilliantly lighted, most tastefully decorated, and filled to its utmost capacity by the *elite* of the district, while the whole entertainment exceeded our most sanguine expectations.

The singing of the Misses Culverwell was exquisite. Their rendering of "The Valley of Chamouni" was perfect, and displayed good taste and considerable cultivation.

Mrs. Cozzens performed her part admirably.

The Misses Fraser presided at the piano in a manner which fully justifies their high reputation; and we have no hesitation in stating that in our opinion Miss Fraser is the best amateur pianist we have heard.

Mr. Boulton exceeded himself on this occasion.

Messrs. Wray, Richardson, Kirk, Walters and Dr. Bridgland, added much to the pleasure of the evening; and the Messrs. Portas won golden opinions for their excellent rendering of the "Larboard Watch," &c. Altogether, a great treat was enjoyed, and should our Newmarket and Barrie friends visit us again, we can promise them a full house, and a hearty welcome.

The building fund has been augmented over $40 by the concert.

WESLAYAN SOCIAL.

The third social of the season, under the auspices of the "Ladies' Aid Society," was given by Mrs. Wm. Kennedy at the Orange Hall, Bracebridge, on Tuesday evening. The attendance was larger than on any former occasion; and the proceeds amounted to over $15, so that numerically and financially it was a great success.

The programme was varied and attractive, and gave the most unqualified satisfaction. The Misses Webster acquitted themselves admirably. Mr. and Mrs. Speer never gave greater satisfaction than on this occasion. Mrs. Burden, Mrs. Tomlin, and Miss Slater added very much to the enjoyment of the evening.

Mr. R.J. Bell, Mr. Long, Mr. Astley, Mr. Griffith, Mr. Russell, Mr. Macaulay, Mr. May, Mr. Burden and others, also took part in the meeting.

A vote of thanks was unanimously given to Mrs. Ross for the use of her excellent piano.

The next social will be given by Mrs. Clerihue, and Mrs. Speer, on the 7th February, in the same place.

GAME.

The lovers of sport may here find ample scope for enjoying themselves, as game abounds all through the District. Deer is exceedingly plentiful. Some of my neighbours have shot as many as nine each in a single day. Partridge is abundant, and the quality excellent. Rabbits also are numerous.

Some time since, Mr. James F. Haines killed a large moose deer near Vernon Lake, which stood from hoof to fore shoulder 18 hands high, and measured around the breast 6 feet 8 inches, while it was 8 feet 4 inches from head to tail; the head from tip of the nose to the ears was 3 feet, and the noble animal carried a pair of very large horns.

In November last I had the good fortune to join in the hunting expedition which took place at Prospect lake, the property of Colonel Maude, C.B., V.C.

The first day the weather was rather unfavourable, but on the second it was all that could be desired.

The gallant Colonel had all his arrangements most complete, and little did the party think when they started that so grand a reception awaited them, or that they would enjoy so rich a treat. As to the *sport*, it was splendid, and far exceeded the expectations of the most sanguine. A good supply of beaver, mink and deer awarded the toil of those who took part in the chase. One young buck weighing over 160 lbs., shot by Mr. J. Long, was very fat and exceedingly handsome, indeed it was the greatest beauty we ever saw. The head of this lovely creature is being stuffed by Mr. Chas. Bard of this place, and will be preserved in commemoration of this gala occasion.

Colonel Maude may well feel proud of Prospect lake. It is truly beautiful, while the country around forms a hunting ground which is unsurpassed in the Muskoka district. The Colonel evidently is a man of progress. Considerable improvements have already been made, and his settlement in Draper is hailed with delight by all the inhabitants.

FISHING.

Our rivers abound with speckled trout, and our lakes with the finest quality of fish, such as bass, pickerel, white fish, and herrings. Salmon trout is also very plentiful in some of our lakes.

WINTER EMPLOYMENT.

Many of my readers may be anxious to know what the settlers do during the winter months, when the snow is deep. For the information of such I may state that the principal part of the chopping is done then, and further improvements effected, while some hire out at the lumbering shanties and earn good wages, to enable them to stay at home and work their farms during the summer.

> "Now in the primal woods the axe resounds,
> And the tall pine receives its mortal wounds,
> As stroke on stroke disturbs the silent snow,
> The wound enlarges by each well-aimed blow.
> The forest giant shakes in all his might,
> And crashing falls beneath his dispoised weight,
> And quickly carries to the branches bent,
> That strive in vain to stop his sure descent,
> A swift and certain ruin with rebound,
> And echoing woods repeat the thundering sound.
> Stript of his limbs, and squared, and hewn he lies,
> To human kind a good but hard-won prize.
> It soon is made to raise the sheltering house,
> Or o'er the seas afar is doomed to roam,
> To build the bark, or to adorn the hall,
> Raised from the ruins of a forest fall.
> His roots remain to meet a slow decay,
> And mend the soil when sown some future day."

EXTRACTS FROM
THE SURVEYOR'S REPORTS

I have thought it desirable to furnish extracts from the surveyor's reports, in order to give my readers a correct and, as far as possible, impartial description of the country.

MORRISON.

Partly bounded on the south-west by the river Severn and Sparrow lake, and to the north by the township of Muskoka, contains 48,519 acres, including water and roads. It was subdivided into farm lots by P.L.S. J.O. Browne, in 1860.

EXTRACT FROM THE SURVEYOR'S REPORT.

"The township, upon the whole, presents a fine field for settlement, as is witnessed by the number of squatters who have made improvements upon the land. The soil is varied both in surface and quality, generally intersected by ridges having a bearing from north-west to south-east, and of more or less abruptness as they approach the deep channels of the lakes and rivers, or have been denuded and covered by alluvial soil in the flats and valleys which intervene.

"The most rugged and unfavourable portion of the land is in the north and north-west portions of the township. The north-east shore of Leg Lake, and some parts of Lake Kah-she-she-Bog-a-mog, flanked by steep bluffs dipping down into deep water, and producing a stunted growth of dwarf oak, birch and inferior pine. The subjacent rock is gneiss, traversed by intrusive veins of highly crystalized granite and pure quartz, and passing gradually into micha schyst and clay-slate. The dip of the strata, where exposed, is from 30° to 45° to the east.

"On the more exposed ridges, in several parts of the township, there appears strong indications of iron and copper ore of much purity. The spots on which I more particularly observed these, are on lot 16 in concession A; lot 5 in concession 6; and to the north of concession line 1 and 2, about lots 30 and 31.

"Approaching the southern portion of the township, the land gradually improves, and particularly upon the eastern shore of Sparrow Lake and the River Severn, and the River Kah-she-she-Bog-a-mog on the western side, and upon the southern and some parts of the eastern portion of the east side, there is a good breadth of excellent land, producing a prolific growth of valuable timber, with indigenous white clover and nutritious grass. This last named description of land extends into Ryde upon the east, and into the unsurveyed portion of Rama on the south. The latter I cursorily explored, whilst fetching a canoe up the Black River, which intersects it for about five miles on the south, and I believe that it would not only be highly favourable to cultivation, but would materially aid the settlement of the southern and eastern district of the Township of Morrison, if it were opened for sale, as it would afford access to the land which I have described above, on which, to my knowledge, settlers have been deterred from improving by want of access through the wilderness which now intervenes between it and the surveyed land.

"A very favourable feature in the topography of the district, is the extent of water by which it is traversed, affording with little interruption, in its unimproved state, an unbroken chain of communication from either extremity of the township to the other, and abounding in excellent fish.

"Upon the upper lakes, and the River Kah-she-she-Bog-a-mog, there are several falls well adapted for Mill sites.

"The central portion of the east side is much occupied by large beaver ponds, which at present obstruct the natural drainage of the country, and drown much otherwise available land. The effect of settlement would be the immediate retreat of the beaver and the destruction of their dams, which would drain down wide breadths of land naturally productive of valuable crops."

DRAPER

Is situated to the east of the Severn and Muskoka Road, the Township of Muskoka lying on the south-east boundary and contains 44,550 acres, including water and roads, of which 20,000 acres, including water and roads, were subdivided by P.L.S. John K. Roche, in 1858. The following is an extract from the Report of Survey:

"The Township of Draper is very well situated in regard to water and mill privileges, the Muskoka River flowing through the township, upon which there is an abundance of power; and, in addition, it is cut up in every direction by streams and beaver ponds, possessing capabilities of being turned to useful purposes.

"The surface of the township is generally hilly, undulating and rolling, and very much so towards the south-eastern part; the granite rock shows itself near to the surface in most parts, and there is a total absence of limestone throughout. The soil is principally composed of a sandy loam, in many instances covered with a rich black mould, and in the north-west part of the Township we found a clay subsoil, but sandy loam is the prevailing soil, and, where it is sufficiently deep, will produce excellent crops. The granite rock, in general, is too near the surface to favor the township for agricultural purposes, though I have no doubt a settlement will soon form, as there is a fair proportion of good land adjoining the centre line in the valley of the Muskoka River, and about the north-west corner of the township, where good clay land is to be found.

"The timber consists principally of hemlock, maple, beech, balsam, tamarac and pine, the latter inferior in quality and not suitable for merchantable purposes. A small proportion of cedar is found in the swamps and very few oaks throughout the township."

MACAULAY,

On the North Branch of the Muskoka River, contains about 41,902 acres, of which 26,000 acres have been subdivided into farm lots, including water and roads, surveyed by Provl. Land Surveyor, John Ryan, in 1857.

"Of the portion of the Township surveyed, the soil generally is good clay—in some cases, a sandy loam—growing a very fine quality of hardwood, with but very few good Pines; a considerable portion of the land is rocky, or strewed—in detached patches—with boulders, but is not, upon the whole, inferior in general character to that of the Southerly and Westerly boundaries, &c.

"As far as has been observed and could be judged, the portion left unsurveyed is either too rocky or swampy and unfit for settlement, at least for the present.

"From the Survey and examinations made, I incline to the opinion that some improvement in the character of the soil may be found to the eastward of Macaulay, and may be sought for, with better prospect of success in that direction, than in those of the other boundaries."

MUSKOKA,

Bounded on the South-west by the River Severn, and on the North by Lake and River Muskoka, and partly subdivided into farm lots by P.L.S. Rankin, in 1857, contains about 32,540 acres, of which 23,945 acres have been subdivided into farm lots, including water and roads. The Muskoka Road runs in a Northeasterly direction through the Township. The following extract is taken from Mr. Rankin's Report of Survey:

"I have to report, that for the purpose of forming a settlement from the Severn to connect with Bell's Line to the Ottawa, a sufficiency of good land is found, so far as this township is concerned, lying in a tolerably direct route from near its S.-W. corner to the Great Falls of Muskoka, viz.: up, or near the side road between lots 20 and 21, to the near the top of the 4th Concession, and thence along or near to the line by P.L.S. Unwin, leading directly to the Fall, where there is abundant water-power for mills or any other sort of machinery, and in the neighborhood of which there is much excellent Pine.

"As to the character and general features of this part of the country, I need only briefly observe, that the rocky ridges (granite) lie generally N.-E. and S.-W., and are of greater or less elevation and ruggedness,—by far the worst part of the township in this respect being within the limits of the first three Concessions.

"The shore of the lake also is, almost throughout, rocky and rough.

"The best part of the township, and where the largest portions, together, of good land fit for settlement are found, is the N.-E. part, bordering on the Muskoka River in both its branches, along the Beaver River, and around the head of Muskoka Bay.

"Some of the larger swamps, on being cleared up, and the Beaver Dams, which back water on them taken away, will no doubt prove desirable for cultivation.

"The only stream (except the Muskoka River itself) of any note is the Beaver River, and that gets very low in summer.

"No mill sites, except that at Muskoka Falls, were observed.

"The Lake abounds in Islands—mostly clumps of rock, though generally timbered.

"The fish caught here are pickerel and bass in the summer; white fish and trout, as I am informed, in the autumn."

WATT

Is situated in the county of Simcoe. It is bounded on the north by the township of Cardwell and Skeleton Lake, on the east by the township of Stephenson, on the south by the township of

Monck, and on the west by Lake Rosseau. It was surveyed in 1865, by Provincial Land Surveyor T.W. Nash, and contains an area of 48,856 acres, including water and roads.

The following is an extract from Mr. Nash's report of survey:—

"The soil of this township has a local reputation of being the best along the Parry Sound Road. The valleys furnish a rich clay loam, in some places inclined to sandy loam; in the high parts the land is not so good, being light sandy soil.

"The good land is found in the valleys in all the parts of the township in larger or smaller tracts, there being but few lots but what have some on; perhaps the valley of Three Mile Lake contains the best lots in the township, there is however much good land near Lake Rosseau.

"The land taken by squatters is generally all good, some of the best lots, however, are still vacant. The poorest portion of the township is that north-east of the Parry Sound road lots, and that adjacent to the northern boundary, the fourteenth concession being mostly broken land. The shores of the waters are mostly lined with hemlock and scrubby pine, maple, balsam, pine and birch are found in all parts of the township, beech is found on the high sandy soils; the pine is not found in groves, so that no portion of the township contains sufficient to reserve for timbering, but it is scattered pretty equally throughout the township, the best perhaps being on the portage from Lake Rosseau to Three Mile Lake, the largest found were about 3½ to 4 feet diameter.

"WATERS.

"The water system is that of the Muskoka River, the whole drainage being to the west, into Lake Rosseau, then by Muskoka Lake and River into Georgian Bay. The surfaces of the lakes are about 100 feet below the main level of the country, and in many places have precipitous banks. Mill seats were found on lots No. 30, con. 1; No 13, con. 4; No. 24, con. 8; No. 42, con. A.

"ADVANTAGES AND PROSPECTS OF SETTLEMENT.

"The very best means of developing the resources of this township and neighbourhood is that already adopted by Government, by improving the Parry Sound road; this road effectually opens up the whole of this township for settlement as well as most of the country immediately north and east of Lake Rosseau; it possesses besides, military considerations of some importance, as it affords military access to the defensive harbour of Parry Sound."

THE FRIENDS OF THE EMIGRANT.

Amongst the list of noble men who have taken a deep interest in emigration, we must give a prominent place to the Rev. A. Styleman Herring, B.A., Incumbent of St. Paul's, Clerkenwell, London. For many years he has been engaged in this benevolent work, and has been instrumental in assisting hundreds to come to our shores. We shall never forget with what pleasure he was met, on his arrival in our village, by some of the emigrants that he had been instrumental in sending to this country; and at the public meeting held in honor of Attorney-General and party, when Mr. Herring was called upon to reply, how gratefully he acknowledged his gratitude to Almighty God for having put it into his heart to engage in this good work. Well might his parishioners give him a welcome on his return home, and present him with a handsome testimonial. He is a noble man, engaged in a noble work. By words of comfort and acts of kindness, he has endeared himself to many in the settlement.

The Hon. Mrs. Hobart, of London (England), has also been doing a good work.

The Hon. John Carling, Commissioner of Public Works, in his Annual Report for 1870, states that "during the past season, Colonel F.C. Maude, R.A., and the Rev. A. Styleman Herring, Vicar of Clerkenwell, London, both active members of Colonial

Emigrant Aid Societies, have visited this Province for the purpose of ascertaining from personal observation, and from intercourse with the large number of emigrants which they had been instrumental in sending out, the condition of such in this their new field of labour. These gentlemen visited the cities and various towns in the Province, and addressed meetings of immigrants in Toronto, Ottawa, and other places, and everywhere received the most grateful acknowledgments from the immigrants for having assisted them to this country, where they are not only able to support themselves and their families, but in many instances already to provide themselves with freehold homesteads in the cities and towns, or in the Free Grant Districts of the Province. In addition to visiting many other sections, these gentlemen made an extended tour through the Muskoka District, with which they expressed themselves highly pleased, seeing in it a section well calculated to furnish homes for the now distressed but steady and industrious working classes of the Old Country."

It affords us great pleasure to add, that Colonel Maude has been so well pleased with the Free Grant Lands, that he has purchased a farm in the Township of Draper, in the District of Muskoka, and decided to become a permanent resident. Following notice is from the *Northern Advocate* of the 28th of October, 1870:

COLONEL MAUDE, C.B., V.C.

This gentleman, we are happy to state, has not only taken a very deep interest in emigration in London, England, but since his arrival in Canada has been so favorably impressed with the country that he has decided to make it his home. With this object in view he has purchased the Prospect Lake property, and is now making the necessary preparations for building a suitable house for a family residence.

Prospect lake is situated on the south-east corner of the township of Draper, 11 miles east of Gravenhurst, and 12 miles from Bracebridge. The Peterson road runs through the north part of the farm, so that he has the benefit of a good leading colonization road to his very door, which is a great advantage; while at the same time it forms the best hunting ground in the district, from the fact that there is no settlement south of his property, Ryde Township not being in market. The writer was on the spot a few days ago, and found partridge, duck, deer, etc., in great abundance.

The gallant Colonel, in our opinion, has made the best speculation that has ever been made in Muskoka. We wish him much success.

EMIGRATION AND IMMIGRATION.
(To the Editor of the "Northern Advocate.")

Sir,—My object in visiting your hospitable shores was to ascertain FOR MYSELF whether my emigrant friends were progressing satisfactorily. Most glad am I to be able to report favorably.

Some few have undoubtedly signally failed, but it is through their own misconduct or by unforeseen circumstances, but to the honest, persevering, *above all* to the sober, Canada affords ample opportunities for advancement. I am informed 40,000 emigrants have settled in the Dominion during the past two years. Yesterday I met here a man earning $20 per week, sometimes $5 per day, who previous to emigration, was eighteen months almost out of work. Who will gainsay the benefit *to all parties*, of such an emigration?

Great Britain has thousands of good charactered persons, able and willing to work, but cannot now obtain it. Why not induce them to move here, and thereby add strength to the Dominion?

I am encouraged to entertain strong hopes that the Government will liberally respond to the almost universal voice of public opinion and put forth more powerful means of attracting and perhaps aiding, the honest, industrious and sober to locate within this favored Dominion.

Population and wealth generally go hand in hand, and Canada greatly requires the one, and the other will speedily follow.

Canada was never so prosperous as at the present moment. Let the Government of the Dominion; the municipal authorities and private individuals, EACH, nobly and liberally forward on this movement, which must inevitably lead to most beneficial results to the whole community.

A word to my emigrant friends:—After having travelled from Quebec to Sarnia, from Parry Sound to Niagara, visited many emigrants at their home, *the grant districts* (100,000 acres of which have been taken up for settlement since April last) and Eastern Townships, I am more and more convinced of the blessings of Emigration.

I find those who care for your souls are zealous, the school system excellent, land and the necessaries of life cheap, and labor good. To all of you I say, "Go forward," (Exodus 14–15.) Do not look back too much on the gloomy past, but look hopefully forward to the future. Avoid murmuring—(1) Keep to your churches. (2) Keep from the whiskey, the curse of this land, woe be to any Legislature which encourages the multiplication of liquor shops. (3.) Keep care of your cents and dollars. Establish "Emigrant Aid Societies," which aim at giving advice to those newly arrived from the old country, a savings bank, a labor mart for hirers and those requiring work—sick and medical clubs— getting out relatives by weekly payments, &c. The Ottawa Society is flourishing. J. Johnson, Esq., Department of Agriculture, Ottawa, will gladly forward their prospectus.

I beg publicly to express my gratitude to the Messrs. Allan (Montreal Steamship Co.) for their considerate and liberal treatment of my emigrants.

I shall carry home (whither I proceed in a few days, after 12,000 miles of travel) the happy feeling that many who in the old country were in poverty and misery, are now by the blessing of God comparatively in a state of happiness, contentment, and comfort.

I tender my most heartfelt thanks to all parties for the many acts of kindness and hospitality I have received from many dear and valued friends, and I shall ever pray God will abundantly bless and prosper the people of this country.

I remain, sir, your obedient servant,

A. STYLEMAN HERRING,

St. Pauls, Clerkenwell, London.

Ottawa, October 25.

THE ONTARIO GOVERNMENT VISIT MUSKOKA.

The members of the Ontario Government and other celebrities visited the Free Grant Districts. I have pleasure in inserting the following, copied from the *Northern Advocate* published at Bracebridge, Muskoka.

On the 14th Sept., 1870, Bracebridge was visited by the Hon. John S. Macdonald, Attorney-General; the Hon. S. Richards, Commissioner of Crown Lands; the Hon. John Carling, Commissioner of Public Works; the Rev. A.S. Herring, B.A., Incumbent of Clerkenwell, London (England); Charles Marshall, Esq., London (England); Fred. Cumberland, Esq., M.P.P.; Wm. Lount, Esq., M.P.P.; A.P. Cockburn, Esq., M.P.P.; the Hon. Sidney Smith, John A. Donaldson, Esq., and a number of distinguished persons.

On the day of their arrival, the villagers got a hint of their intended visit, and resolved to give them a reception. Immense bonfires were kindled on the banks of the river just as the steamer "Wenonah" approached the wharf, and the effect produced by those illuminations was grand beyond description. A large concourse of people assembled at the landing, and gave the company three of as hearty cheers as ever greeted the ear of mortal. The party were then conveyed to the "Dominion House," where a splendid entertainment was got up by Mr. Ross, the well known host.

The chair was occupied by John Teviotdale, Esq., Reeve of the United Townships of Draper, Macaulay, Stephenson, etc., and the vice-chair by Robert E. Perry, Esq.

After ample justice had been done to the good things provided, the chairman rose and proposed the first toast "the Queen," which was drank with all honours; this was followed by "the Governor and Lieutenant-Governors of the Dominion of Canada," which was most enthusiastically received.

Next came "the Army and Navy," which was responded to by Wm. Lount, Esq., M.P.P., in a humorous speech. Mr. Lount concluded with expressing his strong disapprobation of the manner in which the Dominion Government had treated those brave men who were prepared at whatever sacrifice to defend our homes.

"The Ontario Government" was then proposed, to which the Hon. Mr. Macdonald replied. He stated that when he left Toronto he had no idea that such a reception awaited him. The great object he had in visiting Muskoka was, to examine the surface of the country; and he was surprised to find such a crowd of persons congregated to welcome him. He took a deep interest in the prosperity and development of the North, and hoped that the day was not far distant when this section would be as flourishing as those townships on our frontier. He concluded that the credit of settling up our wild lands was due to his Government, that the policy he had adopted was experimental and worked well. The present Government he contended was a Government of the people, not of party; their object was to advance the best interests of country, not of party. He intimated that they had a large surplus of money to be disposed of, and stated that upon all reasonable representations he would give us a helping hand. He contended that he had introduced a greater number of reforms, and established a system of economy, such as no former Government could lay claim to, and made an able defence of the course he had pursued since the coalition.

"Our Guests" was replied to by the Hon. S. Richards, who said that it was not the want of interest in Muskoka that prevented him from visiting it before this, but his duties, public and private, were so enormous that he found it impossible to get away, and concluded by wishing the settlement continued success.

Success to the Emigration Societies of old England. This toast was ably responded to by the Rev. A. Styleman Herring, who said that he was very thankful that God had put it into his heart to engage in this good work, and was rejoiced to find that here the over-crowded population of England could find employment at high wages, and vastly improve their circumstances. He had frequent opportunities since his arrival of conversing with those who had been transplanted to Canada, and he found that they had been vastly benefited in their circumstances by the change; and he was perfectly satisfied that those emigrants who were sober and industrious would succeed.

Success to the Toronto, Simcoe and Muskoka Junction Railway was drank with great enthusiasm, and ably responded to by Mr. Cumberland, M.P.P. In his reply he remarked that he felt that he was surrounded by friends, and was glad to be in a position to state that the building of the road was now a *fixed fact.* His mission to England had been entirely successful, and the stockholders were willing not only to embark in the undertaking, but manifested much sympathy in the object. At first some persons were ready to doubt the sincerity of those engaged in this extension; but the men who took hold of this enterprise were thoroughly in earnest, and were possessed of courage and perseverance, and blessed with means to carry on to a successful completion of any undertaking in which they embarked. He desired

to speak out honestly, and to be distinctly understood in reference to this scheme. He considered that the road to Washago
would be a paying investment for the shareholders; but beyond
that point it would not be so for some time to come; however,
they were prepared to give pound for pound of what it would
cost to build the road from Washago to Bracebridge. He was
pleased to see so much interest taken in the Free Grant Districts
by the Ontario Government, and felt confident that if a Railway
was built to Bracebridge, *two* years would accomplish for this
Section what it would require *twenty* years under the present
system to effect. Considering this, he was satisfied that the Government would render reasonable assistance, as it was eminently
calculated to further the interests of emigration, and raise the
Districts into a position, whereby they would become a source
of enrichment to our flourishing Dominion. He concluded by
stating that if the Municipalities did their duty the road would
certainly be completed as quickly as labor and capital could
accomplish the task.

Mr. Teviotdale on being called, rose and stated, that we would
be gainers by giving a bonus to the Railway, for at present we
had to pay indirectly large sums for freight on goods that would
be greatly reduced when Railway communication was established.

The Health of Mr. Teviotdale, *Reeve of Bracebridge*, was then
proposed by the Hon. John S. Macdonald, and drank with all
honors.

Prosperity to the Free Grant Districts, was replied to by Mr.
Thomas McMurray, who referred to the great improvements
made since he settled in Draper, in 1861, and while giving the
Government great credit for what had been done, he said there
were other things which required legislation: It seemed very
hard that the settler who was at liberty to burn up his pine,
while performing his settlement duties, was prevented from
selling that timber without paying the Government 75 cents a

thousand for the same. He thought that the settler should have the privilege of making the most of whatever timber was upon any land that he was actually clearing, as it would assist him materially in further improvements. Another matter, which deeply affected the interests of the settlers, was the cancellation of arrearages. Now that the District was thrown open to actual settlers on the Free Grant system, those persons who had taken up land prior to the passing of that Act, and had paid one or more instalments, were exceedingly desirous of getting the balance cancelled, and unless this is done, great suffering will be caused to some who have not the means to meet those instalments. He then alluded to the unsafe state of the Registry Offices, and urged the propriety of introducing an Act to authorize the erection of suitable Registry Offices at Bracebridge, Parry Sound, Nipissing and Sault Ste. Marie. He also contended that the formation of the District into a Provisional County, giving us control of our own municipal funds would be a boon to the settlement.

Our Local Member was next toasted, and Mr. A.P. Cockburn, M.P.P., responded.

Next came *the Health* of Mr. Chas. W. Lount, S.M., which was followed by that of Mr. Wm. Lount, M.P.P., who replied in a speech characterized by much eloquence. He believed that this Section would be vastly benefited by the proposed Railway, that the idea of waiting till the country was settled before building a Railroad was a fancy of the past; that now it was seen that where a Railway went settlement immediately followed. He attributed the great success of the United States, to the fact that they encouraged Railroad enterprise, and promised to give all the assistance in his power to procure for the settlers this great boon. He concluded an able speech by stating that he found in Muskoka a superior class of settlers to that of any other new district he had ever visited.

The lumbering interests of the North was ably replied to by John

D. Macaulay, Esq., the popular representative of Messrs. Dodge & Co.

The Health of John A. Donaldson, Esq., *Immigration Agent*, was then proposed and drank with great enthusiasm.

The Commercial and Agricultural Interests of Bracebridge was replied to by Thomas Myers, Esq.

The Press was ably responded to by Chas. Marshall, Esq., (a gentleman from London, England, who is better known to the readers of the "Saturday Review," as Heraclitug Grey.) He expressed the pleasure he had in visiting the Free Grant Districts. He believed that Canada had a great future before her, and that she would yet be the great power upon the American Continent.

The Province of Quebec contains as many square miles as all France; Ontario as many as England, Ireland, Scotland and Wales. New Brunswick is larger than Holland and Belgium; Nova Scotia exceeds England. Columbia has more territory than the whole North German Confederation, together with all the South German States. The North-West is larger than all Russia in Europe, with Sweden, Norway and Denmark counted in, and counted twice over. Besides our vast territory, we were raising a magnificent race of men and women. He thought that Canada had not been sufficiently appreciated by England, and expressed himself delighted with the scenery of our beautiful lakes and rivers.

Success to our American Cousins, was next drank, and ably responded to by Mr. Barker, correspondent of the *Springfield Republican*, who, in his remarks, paid a very high tribute to the firm of Messrs. Dodge & Company, whom he designated one of the wealthiest, and, at the same time, one of the most honourable firms on the American Continent.

"God save the Queen" was then sung, and three rousing cheers given for Her Majesty, after which the company separated.

Next morning the Attorney-General visited the grand Muskoka Falls, and other points of interest. At 11 o'clock the whole company went on board the "Wenonah," and started off amidst the cheers of a vast concourse who had gathered to witness their departure. We understand that on their way to Port Carling, they were entertained at "Maple Grove" by Squire Alport.

FURTHER DEVELOPMENTS.

The great policy of the day is being further developed; and we believe that during the present year much will be done to promote the settlement of our wild lands. Several *new* features have lately presented themselves to the friends of immigration. One is to appoint

BUSHRANGERS.

For years I have advocated the propriety of appointing guides, men capable of leading emigrants through the bush, whose business it would be to see them properly located. For want of this, numbers have been so discouraged that they have left the settlement. If the present Ministry will adopt this course, the comfort of emigrants will be greatly promoted, and the interests of the settlement vastly benefited. Certainly the Government deserve great credit for what they have already done; but here is an opportunity of adding powerfully to the prosperity of the settlement, and I trust that their rigid economy for which they deserve great praise, will not prevent them from taking immediate action in this matter. Suitable men can be obtained, and the benefits which are certain to result, would fully warrant the moderate expenditure required.

Immigration agents should also be appointed, one at Bracebridge, and another at Parry Sound, to attend to emigrants and land seekers on their arrival. How it would smooth the path of the stranger, if, on his landing he was met and seen after by some responsible person acting under the direction and control of the Government. The *Telegraph* says:—

"The indifference of the land, most accessible and easy of observation, is a strong argument in favour of Government appointing

AUTHORIZED AGENTS,

selected from experienced settlers in each district, to point out to intending settlers the most desirable lots, as many in their inexperience select worthless land, and do not discover their mistake until they have spent their money and become discouraged. These agents should not only be prepared to point out the best localities, but also give them practical advice with reference to clearing the ground, the best crops, the easiest means of building their shanties, and various other matters which experience makes so easy."

In addition to this it has been suggested that the Government should cause a certain amount of clearance to be made and a house erected on each lot, so as to have all prepared for the reception of immigrants. The *London Free Press*, in an article on this subject, says:—

"How best to settle the unoccupied lands of Ontario, is a matter not as yet fully determined. Various plans have been tried; and, though they have had their measure of good, yet all the means at command have not been exhausted. The peculiar nature of the lands, and their primitive forest condition, is such as to deter many settlers, unaccustomed as most of them are to forest life, to enter upon them, while the fertile plains of the west offer so tempting a picture. True, the new comer seldom takes into consideration the various elements that collectively constitute Canada a preferable place for continuous abode; its healthful climate; a plentiful supply of pure water; the presence of ample fuel; of timber for building and fencing purposes; to say nothing of the equitable administration of justice, and the general prevalence of law and order. Such advantages too often fail to strike the mind of the European emigrant, whose imagination has been filled with the prospect of fertile prairies, which can be rapidly brought into cultivation. The debilitating fevers, the fitful climate, the scorching sun, followed by deadly dews, are reserved for experience to tell the full force of. The present is too often seized upon by them to the neglect of opportunities lasting in their character, and beneficial in their operation. How best to counteract the tendency alluded to, is a matter worthy of consideration. Many suggestions have been made, but there is one yet to be tried, of which a few words may be said. We refer to the establishment of experimental townships, in which certain preparations shall have been made, so that the settler may find a home ready for himself and family, or such a portion of the forest cleared as will afford him a foot-hold of prosperity. The proposition we desire to advance is, that Government should select some townships, through which roadways should be cut, and on each farm a small house put up, and a small clearing, say of three acres, prepared. One hundred homes might thus be made in each township, the expense of which, and it would not be much, might remain as a charge upon the land. To suitable settlers such farms might be offered by the Government, the only charge being the outlay on the erection and clearing. It would be a great inducement to many to throw their lot with us, if it could be said that, on a lot in such a township a home awaited them; a home which, while it would offer immediate shelter, would at the same time supply the means of immediate subsistence. Private companies have found this plan of procedure to answer well, and lead to the best results. Such an experiment has recently been tried in the State of Maine; a company not only preparing homes in advance, as we have pointed out, but actually bringing over the emigrants free of charge. The country to which they went to seek their population was Sweden; and, by locating people together of similar antecedents, similar language, and, as far as possible, of previous acquaintanceship, the irksomeness of recommencing life, and in the bush, has been wonderfully softened. It has been found in Canada, however, that private land companies have not proved to be continuously advantageous. The aim of such companies has been, in the main, to make money out of their speculations; and hence lands that might have been settled have been held back, or else leased out at an oppressive rental. But the object of our Government is not to be found in a direct money settler. If population is secured the prime end in view is obtained, and thus the chief cause of the failure of enterprises such as we allude to would be removed. It might be well to commence with one experimental township, which could be easily settled out of the incoming immigration; and, if the plan was found to succeed, others would soon be treated in a similar manner. The offer of "One Thousand Homes to One Thousand Families" would attract a vast amount of attention at home, and would lead to organizations among contiguous residents such as has not been seen. If the head of a family had the assurance of the Government agent, that, upon landing at Quebec, he and his little ones would be at once conveyed, free of charge, to a home, half the terrors of emigration would be at once removed. An oppressive uncertainty would be turned into a pleasing assurance, leading up a prosperous future. Thousands would gladly embrace such opportunities. They would be brought face to face with a tangible advantage such as would inspire them with confidence and hope. The fair picture of a prairie home would be dulled by the comparison, and a result would be, that a large portion of the European outflow would be directed here; and another advantage which would ensue would be the permanence of a population so constituted. Once settled in their home they would soon become attached to it, and no thought of roaming would present itself; and this consideration is by no means an unimportant one, seeing that one of the chief difficulties that affects the increase of the population by means of immigration lies in the fact that many who accept the aid the country affords do so only as a stepping-stone to the States. Under the system suggested, this difficulty would be abated, if not altogether removed, and no portion of the general outlay would be lost in helping to build up the neighboring people. We hope, therefore, that some such plan may have a fair trial; and, if it is once successful, it will lead to a change in immigration matters which will be bountifully beneficial.

RELIGIOUS AND EDUCATIONAL.

The religious advantages of Muskoka and Parry Sound far exceed the expectation of strangers unacquainted with the settlement. Visitors not unfrequently entertain the idea that the settlers are shut out from all facilities for the public worship of God, but, happily, it is not so. Religion cultivates a spirit of true sympathy and genuine benevolence, and manifests itself by works of faith and labors of love; it delights in blessing mankind with the knowledge of the Lord, hence love for the souls of men have led to the formation of missionary societies, whereby remote districts are visited with Gospel light. The Methodist Church is peculiarly a missionary church since its formation, the words of the venerable founder, "The world is my parish," has been selected as the motto of his successors, and they are consequently found as the pioneers in almost every new field of labor. The Wesleyan Methodists have the honor of having been the first to sound the Gospel Trumpet in these districts. No sooner had it become known that a Wesleyan family had settled in Draper than the Rev. J.L. Kerr, who was then stationed in Orillia (1861) rode on horse-back 35 miles, to hold Divine Service; nor did he fail to continue to do so until the conference appointed a missionary, namely the Rev. Geo. McNamara, who had the honor of being the first regular Wesleyan minister appointed to this mission. While the Wesleyans were the first to preach the WORD in Muskoka, the Methodist Episcopal Church were the first to appoint a missionary to this mission, because their Conference met earlier then the Wesleyan Conference. The minister appointed by the M.E. Church was the Rev. Gilman Wilson, and we are glad to add that he has continued an actual settler in our midst up till this day. At present the different denominations are well represented. We have in all 12 ministers, comprising 4 Wesleyans, 2 Primitive Methodist, 2 Presbyterians, 3 Church of England, 1 Congregationalist, besides a number of lay agents.

At Bracebridge, we have, a Wesleyan Church, a Presbyterian meeting house, and there is a Church of England close by, so that the inhabitants are well provided with the means of Grace. The following letter from the Rev. Walter Wright, Local Superintendent of Schools, will be read with interest.

GOSHEN LODGE, MUSKOKA FALLS,
December 29th, 1870.
To the Editor of the Northern Advocate.

DEAR SIR,—It would seem to be beyond dispute that the Muskoka Territorial District is making very rapid progress in all matters, civil, commercial, and agricultural,—in everything fitted to promote the temporal prosperity of any people. So speedy, steady, and substantial has this march of progress been, that I suppose it would be difficult to find a fair parallel to it in the entire history of new settlement. I think there has also been a somewhat proportionate progress in things relating to religion, morality, and general education.

1st. In religion, I do not mean that we have had any striking conversions to God, or remarkable revivals of religion. For these we pray, and hope, and wait till God shall send his Holy Spirit abundantly on us as a people. But with the tide of emigration, there have come in among us many truly pious persons, connected with the various denominations of professing christians, and these, added to those who were formerly in the settlement, have helped to elevate the general tone of society. Besides, to meet the spiritual necessities of a largely increased and constantly increasing population, there has been a considerable increase in the number of Christian labourers and means of grace. Several churches have been built, and several others are in contemplation. One leading feature of our religious progress is the great interest everywhere taken in Sabbath schools; and of these we have several, which are both very well attended and very well conducted.

2nd. In morality. Doubtless the influx of new settlers, many of them of a highly respectable and superior class, an increase in the number of true Christians, and a greater number of religious services among us, have all had their influence in raising the standard of general morality. That it is higher than at one time can hardly be doubted. For example, at no very distant date, Sabbath profanation, in various forms, was very common. A great deal of teaming used to be freely done on Sabbath; and I am credibly informed that there were those, in different parts, who would not scruple to log and burn their piles, and do other farm work, on the Lord's Day,—while it was not difficult to procure the means of indulgence in intemperate habits on the Sabbath. Now, these things are almost utterly unknown; and, although there are many confirmed drunkards, and far too much intemperance among us, yet there are several very striking instances of reformation from this worse than beastly vice. I think there is also a manifest improvement in regard to the abominable and degrading habit of profane swearing. Cases of theft are very rare among us. Altogether, our new settlement will compare very favourably, in point of general morality, with any other part of Canada or of the old world.

3rd. In Education, a general and constantly increasing interest is being taken in the education of the youths of our land.

This is shown in various ways. Our county and township

councils give this subject a prominent place in their delibera-
tions and provisions, while our Local press finds room for frequent and extended discussions upon it. The number of schools
in operation has increased during the past year by nearly fifty
per cent.

The aggregate attendance at each of the schools has also
greatly increased. The standard of qualification in teachers is
gradually but surely rising, and there is a very strong desire
cherished by all classes everywhere to have our schools open
during a longer period of the year than has hitherto obtained.
Besides all this, resolutions have been passed and preparations
made for the erection of new school houses in almost every part
of the district. Two very neat and comfortable school houses
have been erected and occupied for some time and others in various stages of preparation, and we have youths among us whose
already proved natural abilities and present attainments give
ground to hope that, with the blessing of God, they may one day
be a credit to Muskoka or to any other land.

I have the honour to be,

Dear Sir,

Yours, very truly,

Walter Wright,

Congregational Minister,

And Located Superintendent of Common Schools for Draper
and Macaulay, &c.

The following we clip from the annual report of the Missionary Society of the Wesleyan Methodist Church in Canada in
1869 and 1870.

MUSKOKA.

It is now eight years since the first Missionary was appointed
by the Wesleyan Conference to this field of labor. Since then,
although Methodism has been slowly but steadily advancing and

increasing in numbers, it was not until last year that it could boast of possessing either Church, Parsonage, or other connexional property of any discription on the Mission. We have now a comfortable Parsonage, which, through the liberal policy of an efficient Board of Trustees, has been partly furnished; also one Church in course of erection, while at several of the appointments our people contemplate building soon. During the past year, most of our congregations have largely increased, while, by the assistance of a second preacher, we have been enabled to take up four new appointments, at each of which we have organized a class. There are now 12 appointments and 11 classes on the Mission. Had we men and means there is yet room and urgent demands for an extension of the work. Immigration has rapidly increased this spring. New settlements are being formed still farther northward in the Free Grant District, from which frequent and earnest invitations are sent to your Missionaries to follow them in and preach to them the Word of Life. We feel deeply for the future prosperity and ultimate success of this portion of our Mission work.

After deducting for 18 deaths, removals, &c., we report a net increase of 52. Members, 121; on trial, 15; Total 136.

S.B. Phillips.

DEDICATION
of the first wesleyan church
in the district of muskoka.

One of the most important events that has taken place in the history of Muskoka, has just been successfully completed. A new Wesleyan Church has been erected in the village of Bracebridge; and was dedicated to the public worship of Almighty God on Sabbath, the 11th December, 1870.

The Rev. F. Berry, chairman of the Barrie District, had the distinguished privilege of officiating on the auspicious occasion, and preached three appropriate sermons to crowded congregations. The presentation was made by Mr. Thomas McMurray, one of the trustees. On the following evening a tea meeting was held for the purpose of liquidating the debt on the edifice. The church was thronged, and a deep interest was taken in the object. Mr. J. Long was appointed chairman, and conducted the meeting with great ability and general satisfaction.

The following gentlemen addressed the meeting:—The Rev. Mr. Gibson, the Rev. Mr. Potter, the Rev. Mr. Mattingly, the Rev. Mr. Webster, the Rev. Mr. Berry, and Mr. Taylor. Mr. James Clerihue read the financial statement, which showed the balance of $350 due on the church, and said that it was desirable that the debt should be wiped out. Mr. McMurray, on being called, stated that an effort would be made to raise the amount due, and hoped that every one present would assist, and thus have the church dedicated *free of debt*. The Rev. Mr. Webster thought that, as this was the *first Wesleyan Church* erected in the district, we should not ask any assistance from the Church Relief Fund, but that we should leave that for those poorer places which had more need of it than Muskoka. Mr. Clerihue and Mr. McMurray then passed round with subscription lists, and returned to the chairman with the gratifying intelligence that the entire amount had been raised; thus the *first* Wesleyan Church in the District of Muskoka has been dedicated *free of debt*. It has been said that "actions speak louder than words;" and we ask those who cry down Muskoka to note this fact that at a tea meeting in the village of Bracebridge, on the 12th December, where the members had previously been heavily taxed towards the erection of the church, when an appeal was made to them for $350 more, in order to have the entire debt removed; the whole amount was subscribed in a few minutes. We trust that outsiders will learn a lesson from this incident.

The music was under the able leadership of Mr. J.H. Speer, Mr. Moorhouse presiding at the organ; and it is not too much to say that the choir performed their part well. The Rev. Mr.

Berry eulogized it exceedingly, and said he never heard better music, nor witnessed greater liberality. We cannot conclude this notice without a special allusion to the address given by Mr. Webster. On rising, he evinced great emotion, and delivered one of the most earnest addresses we ever heard. As the chairman of the district remarked, "he is the right man in the right place;" and the value of his speech may be judged by one remark made by Mr. Berry, namely, that he would not grudge coming all the way from Collingwood to Muskoka to hear the address that he had just delivered.

Votes of thanks were unanimously passed to the Orange body for the use of their Hall, to the Presbyterians for the use of their Meeting-house, to the ladies for the excellent festival, to the choir for their services, and to the chair. The doxology was then sung, and benediction pronounced, and the meeting separated.

Next evening a free tea was given to the Sabbath School children and others, which was also a great success.

"A BLACK PICTURE."

As I have no desire to extol the District, and am anxious to give a fair and impartial account of the settlement, I submit the following controversy, so that my readers may have both sides and draw their own conclusions therefrom.

The St. Mary's *Vidette* of the 27th ult., contains an article under the above heading, which is too rich to let slip the notice of our readers, and in order to furnish them with a little amusement, we give it unabridged:—

"A few days ago, a party of eighteen or twenty farmers from this neighbourhood, having read the glowing newspaper accounts of the free grant lands to the North, started on an expedition to Muskoka, to explore the region for themselves, and see whether it would be advisable for them to move thither. On arriving there, they split up into subsections, each detachment taking a particular field. These traversed the most "promising" townships, examining the soil, consulting the people, taking notes of the landscape, observing the crops, and obtaining all the information possible. After tedious and hopeless wanderings, they one and all returned indignant and disgusted at the imposition of paid agents and rascally speculators; and they declare, in blunt terms, that the idea of its being an agricultural country is a barefaced piece of imposition, invented by tricky sharks, who are fairly coining money out of the necessities of the new comers. These statements have been corroborated in the main by Messrs. John Rouson, Biddulph; Thomas Hughes, Geo. Oliver and Henry Morgan, Nissouri, who have just paid our sanctum a visit on their way home from Muskoka. Three of these gentlemen have themselves travelled through eleven townships, and affirm one and the same story. The soil is nearly all sand and rock, with an occasional spot of clay, while limestone was found only in one small place. The best of the land (a specimen of which was shown us), is a red sort of sand-clay. The water is, for the most part, of the color of strong lye, embittered by balsam and pine roots. Throughout these eleven townships there were about half-a-dozen loads of wheat raised. People who have settled there for seven years past, grow nothing but potatoes—which are really splendid, and come up in double the profusion we see them in Perth or Middlesex. The timber is good, and there is a prodigious lumbering business in the prospective. Pine and birch are very plentiful, but maple and beech are seldom observed. The residents are chiefly emigrants from English cities, who know nothing of farming, and are easily victimized by the Government agents and private adventurers. It is pitiable to see the shifts they are put to in some cases—the brokenheartedness visible upon their features, and the utter wretchedness of their lives. In many cases the remnants of luxury add a kind of ghastly significance to the scene—silk dresses, faded and torn—the remnants of fine carpets, and other mementoes of an easy and comfortable existence among friends in the old country. In short, the narrative accords with the exclamation of one of these returned farmers: "It is the most desperate country a white man ever set his foot on with a notion of settling!" Some of them say they wouldn't take the whole of Muskoka as a gift, if they had to pay the penalty of living out of its soil: and that starvation and rags will haunt the dwellings of settlers as long as they exist. Of course, we know nothing of these things from our own personal knowledge, but it strikes us that there has been a good deal of studied misrepresentation in favor of these lands from time to time. Our informants may, in their present state of mind, look at the blackest side of the picture; but it may do good to people to learn that it *has* a black side. We desire to see every part of Canada turned to good account, but if a section is fitted only for timber and game, it is worse than useless to inveigle farmers into it, in the Quixotic efforts of making it an agricultural country."

The above seems almost too ludicrous to answer, and yet we cannot refrain from a word or two of comment. In the first place, we must congratulate the Government upon the wisdom they have manifested in selecting London as the seat of the Lunatic Asylum, as we have evidence before us that at least, 18 or 20 will shortly be fit subjects for admission into that great institution, and the expenses of removal will not be great. We are not very plentiful in money, but we will give the Editor of the *Vidette* twenty dollars for the photographs of those 18 or 20 men who gave the "black picture" of Muskoka, that we may submit them to the examination of Professor Wells of New York, and have them produced in the *Phrenological Journal*, published by that gentleman. We wish that the Editor had informed us how many days it took those three gentlemen to travel through the eleven township spoken of. We have been told that they never went off the road, and consequently they are incapable of giving an opinion on the subject. We have found that those who take time to examine the country, almost invariably form favorable impressions; while on the other hand, those who run in and run out again, without taking time to explore the district thoroughly, carry away false ideas of the settlement. There is a novelty about the objections raised by the authors of the "black picture," which is refreshing. The water is complained of being "for the most part, of the color of strong lye, embittered by balsam and pine roots," now certainly this is something new; the water has always been praised; all who have ever visited Muskoka, saving and excepting the authors of the "black picture," have admired the clearness, freshness and excellence of the Muskoka water. Have they not "let the cat out of the bag?" We fear they are not all teetotallers, or they would be better judges of pure cold water. The *blackest* thing in the "black picture," however, is the statement, that "throughout these eleven townships, there were about half-a-dozen loads of wheat raised." If this had been the first lie they had told, surely, it would have choked them. They must either be terribly stupid, or mightily proficient in lying. Why, the fact is, Bracebridge flour mill—a mill which would do credit to the flourishing county of Perth— is so full of grists that they can scarcely turn round in it; and every day farmers are coming streaming in with more. This year there was an unusually large quantity under wheat and the yield was good, being from twenty to twenty-five bushels to the acre, and so superior has it been in quality, that visitors have carried away samples of it, declaring that it was better than any they had met with in the front townships. Another libel on our district is embodied in the following sentence:—"People who have settled there for seven years past, grow nothing but potatoes," now we do not believe a word of it; if there is such a case in the district we are not aware of it, and it is exceptionable. As a rule the settlers are progressive and prosperous, and their prospects are bright and cheering.

As another evidence of the utter ignorance of the authors of the "black picture," we quote the following:—"The residents are chiefly emigrants from English cities, who know nothing of farming;" nothing could be farther from the truth than this. There are sections where the English element predominates; but instead of them being in the preponderance, the opposite is the case. The nationality as near as can be is as follows:—One-third Canadian; one-third Protestant North of Ireland people; the remaining third composed of English, Scotch and German. The settlers here can smile at the mock sympathy of the authors of the "black picture." They have all without exception the necessaries of life. Their crops, thank Heaven, were abundant, and prices proved remunerative. Labour is in great demand; working men getting $1 25 per day, and carpenters $1 75 to $2 per day.

In evidence of the general prosperity of the inhabitants, we might just state that not a single application has been made for assistance to our municipal authorities. Those wiseacres say "they would not take the whole of Muskoka as a gift;" but who cares for their opinion? They are not the first who have tried to cry down the country; others, of greater calibre than they can ever expect to be, have spoken and written against it; and yet, despite all the calumny that has been heaped upon it, it grows, it prospers, it thrives. It is not a flying visit to Muskoka that can enable a man to speak with authority on the subject. A district so vast and varied cannot be judged so; but the opinion of those who have lived in the settlement, and grown with its growth, is worth something, and those persons are unanimous in the opinion, that there is from 50 to 70 per cent. of the entire district fit for cultivation, while even the most rocky parts will make good pasture land, and if prosperity is a criterion by which we may judge of the merits of the settlement, then we say that there cannot be found in the Province of Ontario a place giving greater evidence of development and growth than the District of Muskoka, and we venture the opinion that before ten years shall elapse, Muskoka shall be recognized as a place of no ordinary importance. Here we have natural advantages, and water facilities unsurpassed in the world. Near ten years ago, the writer was told by those who had not grasp of mind to see the inevitable future of this important and now rapidly flourishing section, that Muskoka would be deserted; but what is the result? It is filling up with a rapidity unequalled in Canadian history.

Let those fault finders crack the following nut:—There is not to our knowledge in the District of Muskoka a man disposed to leave it, even if money were offered for that purpose. The people like it, and they are happy and contented with their choice; and those who attempt to cry down Muskoka, are not fit to carry drinks to noble pioneers of the North. As to the assertion that "it is the most desperate country a white man ever set foot on with a notion of settling," we need only state that doctors differ. We have lived in it for near ten years, and we like it better every day. It is not a farming country equal to Perth, but there is sufficient land fit for cultivation to make a good settlement, and a prosperous section. The land is given as a free grant. It is easy of access, being within a day's journey of Toronto, and next season a railway will be built into the very heart of the Free Grant District, so that it has its advantages. And certainly to the admirers of nature it is full of attraction. They say "one and all returned indignant and disgusted at the imposition of paid agents, and rascally speculators, who are fairly coining money out of the necessities of the new comers;" now we are at a loss to know who is meant in this wholesale accusation, unless it is designed as a stab at the Crown Lands Agent, the store keepers, and hotel keepers of the district. Mr. Lount is the only paid agent in the place, and it is the first time we have ever heard him accused of trying to induce parties to settle in Muskoka, so the shoe does not fit him. As regards our merchants, they stand as high morally and commercially as those in Perth, and are innocent in the matter, while our hotel keepers are just like all other hotel keepers, they want to make money; but the authors of the "black picture" cannot but say that the fare in Muskoka was both good in quality and plentiful in quantity, while the charges were as moderate as anywhere else. In conclusion, we trust those 18 or 20 will profit by their trip to Muskoka. If they ever go to visit another place, and desire to give publicity to their travels, let them learn to do so correctly; and if Muskoka is so "black" a place in their opinion, let them avail themselves of the supposed superior advantages to be found in Perth, and improve their privileges. We trust they will make better farmers and better husbands by their visit to Muskoka.

THE BLACK PICTURE.

Some time ago we had occasion to refer to a statement which appeared in the St. Mary's *Vidette*, which gave rise to a great deal of discussion with reference to the Free Grant Lands in the districts of Muskoka and Parry Sound.

We regret exceedingly at the one-sided course which the Editor of the *Vidette* has seen fit to pursue in this matter. As far as we know, only one paper, the *Sarnia Observer*, has attempted to coincide with his views, whereas the Press of Ontario has almost unanimously vindicated the fact that there is a large proportion of land fit for settlement throughout these districts.

We know not what character those 18 witnesses bear when they are at home, but we have been told that they commenced their explorations on the Sabbath, and it appears that some of them got on the spree at Port Carling, and one of them fired a gun, whereby the lives of the peaceable inhabitants were endangered, and came near being arrested. They also examined a farm within a mile of this village, lately purchased by Mr. John Elliott, of London township, and ran it down, stating that it was flat rock and sand; now we are in a position to prove that such is a base libel. We know the farm well, and feel satisfied that it would be hard to beat it either in Perth or Middlesex. It contains 213 acres, all hard wood, and is entirely free from stone or flat rock, while the soil is a rich clay loam that cannot be surpassed in quality.

With reference to the insinuation of the *Vidette*, that "the writer of the comments in the *Globe* is probably as ignorant of the district as himself," we are in a position to state that the *Globe* is well posted with reference to the settlement, and is not in the habit of making haphazard assertions. They sent a reporter here who travelled every inch of the ground between Washago and Parry Sound, and that reporter felt the responsibility of the task he had undertaken, and faithfully performed his part. He examined the farms and products of the country—conversed freely with the settlers from lot to lot, and after a thorough investigation, gave a favorable opinion to the world, and if the Editor of *Vidette* will do likewise, he will have cause to write in a different strain of Muskoka, which is not only noted for its beautiful scenery, its intelligent inhabitants, but also for the fertility of its soil. With reference to the imputation thrown at ourselves, namely, "that it is our business to puff our home," and consequently "little dependence can be placed in our statements;" we have just to remark that our business is to *state facts*, this course we have invariably pursued, and with such weapons we have faced much opposition and have always triumphed. We well remember the time when Mr. Simpson's letter appeared, and had it not been for such misrepresentation, probably we would never have taken the stand we took in reference to these settlements; but being thoroughly convinced from personal knowledge and close observation, that there was a large amount of land fit for agricultural purposes, and satisfied from its geographical position and wonderful natural advantages, that before long Muskoka would become one of the most prosperous parts of Ontario, duty prompted us to advocate the settlement of these wild lands; and we think that the past success of the settlement is a sufficient guarantee to those who shall hereafter settle, that with sobriety, patience and industry, success is certain.

If the question is put, Why do you recommend people to settle in Muskoka? we reply: We are acquainted with hundreds in these districts who have been much improved in their circumstances by settling in our midst. Numbers who came here with very small means, and some even without means, now own good farms, which are well stocked, and their circumstances would compare favorably with those outside.

The editor of the *Vidette* tries to excuse himself thus:

"All we can say to this is, that if we have printed the truth, it matters very little to us whether the Premier or any other dignitary suffers by the exposure. If we have not done so, we were, at any rate, warranted in publishing the earnestly-expressed opinions of so many respectable farmers of this neighbourhood, made after a thorough personal observation of the country."

Now, we state, had the truth been printed, we would not have troubled ourselves to reply; but the "Black Picture" is a *black falsehood*, and, in justice to the settlers and the settlement, we were obliged to enter upon the defence.

The amount of evidence in favor of what we have written and said about this country is so voluminous, that we find it difficult to make a selection. However, for the information of our readers, we give a few extracts, and call attention to the letters of the Rev. John Webster, headed "Muskoka calmly considered," which appeared in the two previous issues of the *Advocate*, by which it will be seen that in his opinion there is from 70 to 75 per cent. of the land fit for cultivation. A great deal of weight must be attached to Mr. Webster's statement. He has travelled the length and breadth of the District with a zeal worthy of the great work in which he is engaged, and has had ample opportunities of judging of the country.

The *Globe* says, a short time ago a dark picture was given by the St. Mary's *Vidette* of the state and prospects of the Muskoka region. It seems some farmers from that neighbourhood had gone on a flying visit, and came back with a most dreadful account of what they saw, heard, and tasted. The *Northern Advocate* takes up the cudgels in favour of the maligned region, and point by point meets the representations of the St. Mary's visitors, and with a great deal of earnestness repudiates the representation as a laughable and outrageous caricature. The fact is, the "picture" drawn was so black that it carried its own contradiction on the very face of it. For instance, it was said that in eleven townships "about half a dozen loads of wheat were raised." The *Advocate*, in reply, says that the Bracebridge flourmill alone is so beset with teams bringing and taking away grists, that one can scarcely turn himself. Half a dozen loads for eleven townships would not justify the erection of a flour mill at all. To represent the water of the Muskoka region as a villainous compound, like lye, is also exceedingly foolish, and worse for even the casual visitor can easily know that generally it is exceptionally good. Muskoka may not be all its most sanguine friends have represented it to be, but it is not the waste, howling wilderness the Missouri farmers have pictured, or anything like it. Other people have been there as well as the good friends of Perth, and are quite sure that the picture drawers must have taken heavy suppers, and had unpleasant dreams.

The Beaverton *Expositor* says: the editor of the St. Mary's *Vidette* repeats that personally he knows nothing of Muskoka, and then retorts to the refutation of statements contained in his paper, that they were the "accounts of intelligent and trustworthy farmers who had paid a visit to that region;" while, he asserts the writer of the comments in the *Globe* is probably ignorant of the district as himself, and little dependence can be placed on the *Advocate*, because it is its business to puff its home. We do not suppose our *confrere* has wilfully maligned Muskoka; and his anxiety to defend his friends is not surprising, though the manner in which he does it is. We can assure the *Vidette*, from personal knowledge, that the tale of those "intelligent farmers" is equally as incorrect as were the reports circulated through the American press, during the civil war, and stated to be vouched for by "an intelligent contraband."

The *Orillia Packet* says:—

"At the entrance of the district it has a most forbidding aspect, but there are continual signs of improvement as you go further in. The products of the district are usually of the best quality, and the yield per acre good. It is not claimed that Muskoka is equal to the older parts of the Province, but it is claimed that good land may be obtained there, that the climate is healthful, and the water good and pure, though generally soft. The settlers are, as a class, possessed of more than ordinary intelligence, contented and prospering. They went there for the purpose of securing homes for themselves and families, and this they are doing in a much larger proportion of instances than is the case in most Canadian settlements. We are personally acquainted with not a few who went there with nothing, and now are in comfortably independent circumstances, and there are several really wealthy persons in the district, who have avoided lumber and Government land speculations. In fact, the latter is of comparatively rare occurrence there.

"The story related by the *Vidette* has very little foundation in fact and we are only surprised our *confrere* allowed himself to be so grossly misled by such an eminently ridiculous story, which carries contradiction on the face of it. The greater part of the studied misrepresentation with reference to the District of Muskoka has been the work of the enemies of the settlement; Government agents, there is but one in the District; and the settlers avoid it well knowing that ultimately the result would be adverse to the prosperity of the settlement."

The *Barrie Advance* says:—

"The settlement has a very zealous defender in the editor of the *Advocate*. He is himself one of the pioneers of the District;

and as one who is in a position to know the facts, and of good repute as to credibility, we prefer taking the picture he draws on the subject, to that of the *Vidette*'s eighteen witnesses."

The following appeared in the *Northern Advocate* on the 6th and 13th of January, 1871:

MUSKOKA CALMLY CONSIDERED.
BY THE REV. JOHN WEBSTER.

To the Editor of the "Northern Advocate."

MR. EDITOR.—I wish, through your paper, to place a few thoughts before your readers on this great Muskoka country. The enquiry is frequently made, "What do you think about Muskoka?" Without noticing those questions separately, my friends will find an answer to them in this letter.

The country is variously described by different individuals, according to the stand point from which it is viewed. In my opinion, some place their standard far too high, and others far too low. After having spent nearly six months in the district, I believe a medium view will be more correct, and therefore I shall follow it.

The country is diversified—it is not one great plain, neither is it a mountainous country. We have hills and dales, rocks and lands, rivers and lakes in abundance. The scenery is most beautiful. It would be hard to surpass in loveliness some of those lakes, nestled as they are in an almost unbroken forest, still with enough clearance on their shores to give them a beautiful, wild, romantic appearance. As you sail on those waters, and pass silently around numerous rocky islands, covered with trees, mostly pine and other evergreen trees, as the balsam, spruce, and hemlock; passing now and then an island with one solitary tree standing on it, to brave the buffeting of the storm alone, you imagine you see some of the scenery described in some fairy tale you have read in childhood. But the Christian can, however, turn the whole scenery to a better account, as he reads his Bible, and reads of Christ, the "Rock of Ages," upon which the soul can anchor and be safe, while the storm of life passes over him. Some of the largest islands can be cultivated, having excellent soil on them.

THE ROCK

Generally rises up suddenly and abruptly; some places to a great height, and then sinks down into the ground to unknown depths. It is no uncommon thing to see wells, within a few feet of a great rock, or surrounded with rocks, sunk 30 and 40 feet and not touch the rock. They are in ridges, generally running from southward to northward,—some places extending for several miles, and other places only a short distance. But those rocky ridges are not nearly as extensive as a stranger would imagine, as they are not very wide. There are very few rolling stones in the land; they are only found in a few localities. There is very little flat rock. We have not much swampy land—the rocks of Muskoka seem to take the place of the swamps in the western part of the province.

THE SOIL

Is generally light, being a sandy loam. In some places you may find clay; but it is the exception, not the rule. The soil however is fertile and well adapted to the growth of grass, peas, oats, rye, barley, potatoes, and all kinds of roots, but will never, in my opinion, be a first rate wheat country. In some chance places and seasons you might have a good crop; but it won't pay for the farmer to turn his attention to wheat raising. Stock raising and dairying is what will pay, and pay well. The land being high, dry, and rolling, is admirably adapted for sheep grazing. The farmer, who turns his attention to stock raising, as above mentioned, will, with the blessing of God, I think, succeed and live as comfortably as in almost any other part of Canada. There is, I presume, about 70 or 75 per cent, on an average, of land that can be cultivated. The timber in the forests is pine, hemlock, maple, beech, birch, and in some localities considerable oak.

The spring and well water can be used for washing purposes as satisfactorily as rain water. It is not black and brackish, as some have stated, only where it is affected by minerals. The water in the Muskoka River and Lake is of a darkish color, and in some of the creeks, but the water generally is clear and beautiful. On account of its softness it does not agree with some people when they first come to the district, but when they become used to it the effect it first produced ceases, and they generally like it better than hard water. I will not say that all like the country; but the most of those who settle in it like it very much, and are happy and contented. I would advise any Canadian wishing to "locate land," to come first, spend a few days, look around him; if he can suit himself, select his lot, build his shanty, return and fetch his family and move them at once to their own homes, and thus save them from a great amount of toil, fatigue, and expense.

THE LAND POLICY.

Government has made a pretty liberal land policy, and grants 200 acres to a man having children under 18 years of age, and allows him to purchase a third 100 acres for $50. A young man can draw 100 acres, and purchase the second for $50. By this free grant system many are induced to come out and settle in the district. The Act however needs mending, which I hope will take place at the present session of Parliament. I am not going to embark in politics, Mr. Editor, nor find fault with the Government, or anyone else; but, as a Canadian, I understand Canadian life; and now, as I live in the Muskoka District, I know what the settlers need, and what would be advantageous and beneficial to both the settlers and the Government. I can only name a few, without entering on any particular argument, as I have not room in this paper. I shall notice—

1. The restriction on the pine growing on the land being

cleared for the "settlement duties." While the country should be protected from being stripped by mere speculators, yet the actual settler should not be forced either to burn up the pine on the land he clears, or pay the Government 75 cents per thousand feet if he sells it. Where a man lives a little distance from the water, 75 cents per thousand feet take away his profits, and he cannot afford to draw the logs to any market, consequently he is forced to burn up the most beautiful and valuable pine. He should be allowed to have every stick that grows upon his land; and, while he ought to be restricted and prevented from "stripping" the land of the valuable timber, and not clearing it, yet he should be allowed to sell any timber on the land he clears, fences and prepares for crops. For the want of this privilege, thousands of dollars worth of timber, last summer, was burnt in clearing the land; which was a great loss to the country, and of no benefit to the Government.

2. The restrictions on mines, minerals, &c., should be taken away, and let the owner have all that is in the ground and rocks, as well as what is on them; and if there is anything valuable in them, let the country be developed. If there should be a valuable mine, or mineral of any sort discovered, let it be worked, and pay the Government a tax according to the value received.

3. Another amendment should be made, to allow those settlers who were in the country and drew one hundred acres under the old Act, to draw a second, and thus allow those, who bore the toil, burden and hardships of a new country life, to have at least equal privileges with those coming now into the District.

4. Another is, squatters should be allowed to have their land, and enjoy their clearings, without having to pay for them. Some of them suffered almost everything but death by starvation when they came to the District. Small as their shanties and clearings were, they were made a great blessing to the other settlers coming into the District. They ought to have their lands as free grants. I hope some member of the Government, or some

other gentleman of the House, will bring about these and several other reforms, which this great new country needs to make it what it ought to be.

THE ROADS.

The Government lays out large sums of money yearly in building roads; by this means much has been done towards the settling of this country and giving employment to emigrants. The road from Washago to Gravenhurst lies, for the most part of the way, between two great ridges of rocks, which give the whole country, to a new comer, a barren and frightful appearance. Many persons who are fearful and tender-hearted, return next day, declaring the country is not fit for white men to live in. A large amount of money was spent on this road during the past summer, in grading, planking, gravelling it, and in building bridges. The lakes and rivers are our great highways in the summer season; consequently, off the leading Government roads, the other roads are neglected by the settlers, but they must in a few years be opened out.

EMIGRATION

Is pouring in rapidly. Mr. Lount, the Crown Land Agent, since May last, has located over 100,000 acres of land. The emigrants, both from the old countries and Canada, are generally of the right stamp. I never saw a better class of people settling in any new country. The majority of them are a reading, well educated, industrious people; many of them highly cultivated. With such a class of people, and the blessing of God this part of the country is destined to take, in a few years, a prominent place in the Dominion of Canada.

RELIGION

Is not neglected. There are three Wesleyan ministers, two Primitive Methodist ministers, one Church of England minister, and Congregational minister. The Presbyterians were supplied with students from their college during the summer season. The Church of England have two churches, the Primitive Methodists once church, the Presbyterians one church, and there are three small union churches in the District.

THE PRESS.

The *Globe* says:—

We are glad to notice that the locations in the Free Grant District are increasing in a very gratifying degree. The number of acres taken up during the last three years was 239,732, of which 139,233 were so occupied during 1870. The number of adults over 18 years of age who settled in that region during the same period was 2,021, of whom 1,080 were during the last year. The plan, first suggested we believe by Mr. Donaldson, the Toronto Emigration Agent, of making a small clearance of Free Grant lots and building a house, for which the settlers are to pay, is to be tried in a township selected for the purpose. We cannot but think that it will be a great boon to many a family. It will enable them to bring all their goods and chattels on at once, and allow them to put in more or less of a crop during the first year. We trust that it will be found so successful as to be carried forward vigorously as a part of the regular business of the Department.

The *Daily Telegraph* of December 21, 1870, says:—

THE MUSKOKA DISTRICT.

In the course of the debate on the Address, several members of the Opposition stated that the land in the Muskoka district was unfit for cultivation, and that the Government were acting cruelly and deceitfully in inducing people to settle in such a rocky wilderness. The charge was met by members of the Government and others, who informed the House that, though there certainly were barren tracts in the district, at least 70 per

cent. of the land was fit for cultivation. This statement is fully
borne out by persons who have visited the Free Grant region;
many of them old Canadian farmers in every way capable of
forming an opinion. It is a fact that many Canadians have gone
into the Muskoka District from the older settlements of the
Province, and are doing well there. It is also a fact that hundreds
of immigrants have taken up lots during the last year or two.
Now, when we find all those persons remaining in the district,
and when we find them contented and satisfied, the country
cannot be such a wilderness as some members of the House
would have the public believe. So far as we know, very few persons have abandoned their lots; and complaints from settlers are
seldom heard. They want gravel roads and a railway, in order to
give them connection with our market; and were those wants
supplied, we believe the Muskoka District would rapidly fill up,
and would, in the course of a few years, become one of the finest
settlements in Ontario.

As the following letter, written by a gentleman who has visited the Free Grant District, fully meets the assertions of members of the Opposition, we give it place in these columns:—

"Sir,—Having attended the sittings of the House during the
debate on the Address, I was much surprised at the reckless
manner in which hon. members, and notably Mr. Evans, addressed the House in regard to the condition of the settlers, and
the quality of the land in the Muskoka District. He stated that
it was not fit for agricultural purposes, and infinitely inferior to
the prairie lands in the Western States; that the advantages held
out by the Government of Ontario were not such as to induce a
Canadian farmer to settle in the District; and that there was not
a farmer in Upper Canada who would recommend his son to
take up his residence in Muskoka, with a $500 note to start him-
self, because the Government had power by act of Parliament to
take away every valuable stick of timber on his land if they saw
fit, and no freeman would take up land on such terms. Now, Mr.

Evans cannot have made himself personally acquainted either
with the settlement duties required by the Act of 1868, or with
the Muskoka Territory itself. Having travelled in Muskoka last
summer, and gone, I may say, through a considerable section of
it, I can fully corroborate all the Minister of Agriculture stated
in his reply; but I consider that the latter gentleman did not go
far enough; that he under rather than over valued the resources
of the Free Grant District. Having had a great deal of experience of land in several parts of Great Britain, and having been
out here sufficient time to become acquainted with the capabilities of the Province of Ontario for agricultural purposes, a few
words comparing the Muskoka with others, and enumerating
the advantages it holds out to settlers, may perhaps be interesting to your readers. I may first premise that I never heard one
settler complain of his portion, but all spoke most strongly in
favor of the territory, whether they were shipwrights from the
Thames, farm laborers from Devon or Canadians. The advantages of the Muskoka District, which present themselves most
prominently to my mind, are—

"1. The short distance it is from Toronto, Bracebridge, the
centre of the Free Grant townships, being nearer to it than
London, Canada West; and when the railroad is completed to
Gravenhurst, Bracebridge will be within six hours of Toronto.

"2. The easy means of access by railroad and boat, with a
break of only 14 miles staging over a plank road, for the construction of which last summer the Government appropriated a
large sum of money. When the rail runs through to Gravenhurst
that staging will be avoided.

"3. The easy terms on which a head of a family can acquire at
least 200 acres of good agricultural land, viz: to reside for six
months in each year for five years in his location; to clear fifteen
acres of land during that period; to cultivate at least two acres
yearly and to build a log-hut of certain dimensions.

"From a careful examination of the country, I am convinced

that there is at least 70 per cent. of good agricultural land, and comparing it with Northumberland, Westmoreland, Cumberland, and the adjacent parts of the counties bordering thereon, I am of opinion that the preponderance of Muskoka in good land over the named counties is at least 37 to 40 per cent.; and comparing it also with counties in the south-west of England, such as Cornwall, Devon, Dorset, &c., the result in favor of Muskoka is as 7 to 5. Of course, in an agricultural point of view it does not come up to the midland, eastern and southern shires of England, but on the other hand it has advantages of its own which they do not possess, such as water privileges, &c. As to the idea that the Free Grant District is a mass of rock (though the fact that there is plenty of rock there cannot be denied) is all a mistake. Many of the settlers, however, prefer a portion of rock, as they consider that the rocks retain during the night a large proportion of the heat received from the sun during the day, and, consequently the atmosphere is greatly mellowed, preventing the frosts in the spring and fall from being greatly injurious. The crops that I saw when there promised a good return for the settler's labors, and that promise has been fulfilled. I have seen samples of cereals grown there quite equal to that produced in the best wheat growing townships in Canada. The roads, in consequence of the rock in the district, are in capital condition, and can compare most favourably with those of much older settled districts. That the climate is not severe is proved by the fact that last spring the steamers were running in Muskoka on the 4th of April, while Lake Simcoe was not open for navigation until the 22nd. It is also a mistake that the Free Grant District is so far north, nothing of the kind. The parallel of latitude, which is the boundary line between the eastern townships and Vermont, runs through the Muskoka Lake. In fact, it is in the same latitude as Cornwall, Ontario.

"As to the Government having the right to take the timber as stated by Mr. Evans, it is also a mistake. A settler, if located on a pine lot, is allowed to chop thirty acres during the five years without any license, and after the expiration of the five years all the pine on the lot is absolutely his own. If he wishes to chop more than the thirty acres before he receives his patent, he must pay the same license as a lumberer would have. But, if he is located on a hard-wood lot, there is absolutely no restriction whatever. Again, if a man finds that in his lot there are a certain number of acres unfit for *agricultural* cultivation, he has only to bring two witnesses who will make the necessary affidavit of the fact, and he is entitled to an equal number of acres out of another lot, retaining his own also. In fact, a man has 100 acres of *agricultural* land whether he has only that amount or more.

"I am so perfectly satisfied with the territory and the capabilities it affords of enabling a certain class to get on, that I have written to the old country, advising several parties to come out in the spring, and take up locations in Muskoka; and I have every reason to believe that several will make up their minds to do so. It is not only a farmer who can get on there; for there is almost a representative of every class of persons there. Witness, officers on half pay, jewellers, shipwrights, clerks, painters, weavers, lawyers, &c.

"Apologizing for occupying so much of your valuable space, but the conviction that the resources of the Free Grant Territory are not known as they ought to be in Canada, must be my excuse. A settler going there will find everybody ready to lend him a helping hand, and afford him every information. I know instances of men who settled in that district four or five years ago with almost nothing, and have now good farms, and are happy, contented and prosperous."

Again, the *Telegraph* has the following:—

"THE COLONIZATION ROADS

are doing an immense and plainly perceptible amount of good in increasing immigration, the Hon. Attorney General has pledged that the Government intend still pursuing a liberal policy with reference to the opening up of this district. Nature has done much in clothing this part of the land in beauty, in supplying it with great resources and inducements for immigration, and it only remains for the Government to assist in the development of the Muskoka district.

"As an evidence of the increase of immigration to this Province, we have much pleasure in giving the following from the Hamilton *Spectator* of the 21st January, 1871:

"IMMIGRATION REPORT.

"Mr. Carling is not a show Minister in the debates of the House, but there is an unobtrusive enthusiasm in his management of the affairs of his Department which has already yielded good fruit, and gives promise of more. Above all, there is a praiseworthy punctuality in his dealing with the public which we should like to see imitated by the heads of departments at Ottawa. The present year is but in the first month of its age, and yet we have Mr. Carling's Immigration Report for 1870. From our knowledge of what had been done in this Department, we felt justified in predicting, some time ago, that the immigration for the past year would be greater than it had been in 1869, even though the latter year showed a handsome increase over preceding years. We are glad to find that we have not been disappointed. The total number of immigrants who settled in the Province in 1869, as shown by the reports of Hamilton, Toronto, Kingston and Ottawa agencies, was 15,893. In 1870, the number was 25,290, showing an increase of 9,397. As an evidence of the judicious policy adopted by the Government on this question, and as an illustration of the progress we are making, we give the immigration returns since 1866:

"Number of immigrants settled in Canada in

1866	10,091
1867	14,666

1868 12,765
1869 18,630

"These figures, let it be borne in mind, are for the two Provinces of Upper and Lower Canada previous to Confederation, and for the whole Dominion afterwards. The figures show that the largest number of immigrants in any one year was under 19,000, while last year, for the Province of Ontario alone, it was over 25,000. It may be said, and no doubt will, that more might have been done; but if the numbers were increased a hundred fold that argument would be of equal force, and might be urged with as much fairness as it is now. It should be remembered that a healthy immigration is one that can be readily absorbed by our industrial system. A greater number than is indicated by this test is not desirable in any one year; for, of all things, we must guard against a well-founded discontent among our immigrant population. Even a temporary inconvenience in obtaining employment is certain to cause such discontent, and it is certain to find its way across the ocean, to our future injury.

"With our ever widening area of settlement, it is very true that inconvenience and discomfort from want of employment can be but temporary, and it is equally true that those who are ready to settle upon land may come in almost unlimited numbers; but after all, the great majority of immigrants will be men in want of employment immediately upon landing; the more industrious and energetic of whom will get into better positions in the course of time. How nearly the immigration of 1870 was proportioned to our industrial wants, may be roughly estimated by returns from the municipalities, in answer to Mr. Carling's inquiry as to how many they could find employment for. According to these returns the number asked for was 22,802. It is very certain, of course, that every employer who could find work for a laborer upon his farm, a mechanic in his workshop, or a domestic servant in his home, did not make a statement of his wants to the Government. This number, therefore, it may reasonably be inferred, does not mark the limit of the country's capacity to give employment, but merely expresses the more urgent wants of employers. The number that actually arrived we know considerably exceeded this, for Mr. Carling tells us that "in addition to the number reported from the above (Ontario) agencies, there has doubtless been a large accession to the Province of settlers from Great Britain and Ireland, who paid their own expenses out, and of whom we have no available record as to their numbers." These, he thinks, with the arrivals reported at the four agencies, probably sum up to a total of not less than 50,000 souls added to our population by immigration for the two years 1869 and 1870. The fact that all these have found employment among us without in the least affecting the labor market, is a most gratifying proof of the prosperity which the country at present enjoys. Each one of them will create employment for others who are to follow, and if the change has been a satisfactory one to them—as we know to be the fact in nineteen cases out of twenty, at least—each will become an immigration agent within his own circle of friends at "home," co-operating with the other agencies at work, and helping us to solve what, after all, is the grand problem for Canada—the settlement of the country.

"There can be no doubt that when the Government selected Mr. White as Emigration Commissioner to England they did an inestimable service to this Province. We have heard same carping criticism—of the perfunctory and professional kind—upon Mr. White's mission: he didn't go at the right time of the year; he didn't stay a sufficient length of time, and he didn't go into the agricultural districts—with other stuff of the same kind. But he did something far more important than all these; he did, in fact, the one thing needful to be done at the time; he caught the public ear on the emigration question, made it a subject of popular discussion, and enlisted in its behalf the efforts of philanthropists, and these efforts are now bearing fruit.

"Encouraged by past success, Mr. Carling proposes to enter upon an experimental field. He recommends that a township be set apart from among the back townships of the Free Grant district, containing good agricultural lands, and an appropriation made sufficient to enable the Government to make a clearance on alternate lots, to the extent of from three to five acres, and erect a log house thereon; these to be given to heads of families of good character, with the cost of the Government improvements as a first charge upon the land, and to be repaid in instalments during the 3rd, 4th and 5th years of settlement. This is spoken of as but an experiment, and it is just possible that there may be found many practical difficulties in carrying it out; but it is well worth trying, and if it be guided to success its value will be very great."

The Rev. Dr. Newton writes:—

"I have great faith in the bright future of this country. My duties as a clergyman necessitate an extensive and familiar knowledge of the people and the District of Rosseau and Nipissing, and I am glad to bear witness to much contentment and prosperity among sober and industrious settlers. Many who came in with very little, are quietly making comfortable homes, and realizing property. And observe the longer they live here the better they like the country."

The publisher has much pleasure in presenting the following letter, which he has received from R.J. Oliver, Esq., late Crown Lands Agent for the District of Muskoka:

"St. Louis, Mo., U.S.,
"18th January, 1871.
"Thomas McMurray, Esq.,

"Dear Sir,—I have read with interest the Prospectus of your History of Muskoka, soon to be published in pamphlet form. For some time past I have been arranging my notes on the settlement, with the view of publishing them, but am very much pleased to be superseded by one so well qualified for the work. Your long residence in the settlement, dating from within a few months of its opening to the present time, gave you every opportunity for collecting such information as you may need, and I know you have not been a sleepy observer of passing events.

"*The constant influx of land seekers to my office through your agency, during your itinerancy in the Temperance cause, leave testimony to your untiring zeal in the welfare of your adopted country*, and now that you have the press at your command, full scope can be given to the genius and power of your mind. The information you promise to give is much needed abroad. Canada has long been most shamefully misrepresented by interested and competing parties, and a compendium of facts coming direct from the settlers, not bearing the authority of speculative organization, will be received without suspicion, and consequently a much stronger tide of immigration may be expected to flow into the vast Free Grant Districts of Canada.

"Since my residence in the States, I have made it my special object to inquire into the condition of settling on prairie lands, and my conclusion is that *a person with limited means can make a home* on bush land in Canada, at half the cost; with better chances for success, and with much more comfort than can be obtained on the bleak tree-less prairies of the Western States. I speak advisedly and from personal observation and inquiry.

"Hoping that your laudable enterprise may be fully sustained.

"I am, yours, &c.,

"R.J. OLIVER."

THE SETTLER'S GREATEST ENEMY

I cannot conclude this book without giving a word of warning to those who are in the habit of tampering with strong drink. It has been my painful duty to record the sad havoc which drink has caused in the settlement since my arrival; and as I do not wish to be personal, I will simply state that not a few farms have been lost on account of intemperance. Some of the first settlers, in consequence of it, have been obliged to quit the settlement after considerable improvements had been made, and not a few deaths have been caused by indulgence in the seductive practice of drinking. It matters not where we turn—as in the city so in the backwoods—drink is the common enemy of man. If I should lift the veil, and relate what I have *known* and *witnessed* of drink's doings in Muskoka, it would fill a volume larger than the present one. Drinking is the road to ruin, and we tremble for those who are walking thereon. Some that we love and respect are on the very verge of the precipice, and sad to relate, they seem ignorant of their danger. Stop! I cry, or your fate, like some who have already perished, will be sad and terrible. Drink is alike injurious both to buyer and seller, and its victims have been made up of both classes. Many of my friends and supporters are engaged in the business, but while I hate the traffic, I entertain no unkind feelings towards the men. My worst wish is that they would engage in some other calling, or banish the liquor from the bar.

RAILWAY TO BRACEBRIDGE.

The following petition, signed by over one thousand settlers, was presented to the Ontario Government:

"PETITION

"To the Honourable the Legislative Assembly of Ontario, in Parliament assembled.

"The petition of the undersigned, settlers of the District of Muskoka, humbly sheweth:—

"I. That railroad communication is much required by the settlers, and, in order to promote the development of the district, it is an absolute necessity:

"II. That the interests of immigration would be largely promoted by an extension of the Toronto, Simcoe, and Muskoka Junction Railway through the Free Grant territory:

"III. That apart from all local considerations, the Province would be largely benefited by promoting this scheme, from the fact that there is still unoccupied a vast extent of our country, capable of affording homes for at least 200,000 families, that would quickly become settled by a loyal and industrious people if railway facilities were furnished:

"IV. That said company, having accepted tenders for the construction of their road to Washago, your petitioners are of opinion that your honourable body could not expend a portion of the surplus at present in your hands more advantageously than by giving a substantial grant to aid in the extension of this line through the heart of the Free Grant district.

"And your petitioners will, as in duty bound, ever pray, &c."

The *Northern Advocate* of February 24th, 1871, contains the following:—

"RAILWAY BUSINESS.

"We call the attention of our readers to the article which appears in this issue, headed "RAILWAY TO BRACEBRIDGE," by which it will be seen that an arrangement has been entered into to extend the Toronto, Simcoe, and Muskoka Junction Railway right through to Bracebridge. The conditions are the best that possibly could be made, namely, the Government give $4,000 a mile, the Company $10,000, and the District $2,000. On these terms, *and on these alone*, the Company will extend their line from the present terminus—(Thomson and Millar's, Rama)—to Bracebridge; and, unless these conditions are complied with, the Road must stop at Thomson and Millar's.

"The Bonus will be extended over twenty years, and no payment is required unless as sections of the road are completed. By this arrangement the ratepayers will never feel the tax—in fact, they are paying more now in extra freightage twice over than will be required of them by way of assistance in the construction of the road. Besides, when the line is built, the value of property will greatly increase and a vast impetus will be given to business, while the wild lands will quickly be taken up and general prosperity mark our settlement.

"Here we have numerous lakes and rivers which would become tributaries to a railway. Our supplies of timber are almost inexhaustible; our mill privileges are unequalled on the continent; and all we want, to make Muskoka one of the most flourishing parts of Ontario, is railroad extension. Give us this, and our district will become quickly settled, and capitalists will be induced to come in and develop its resources."

RAILWAY TO BRACEBRIDGE.

Realizing the importance of Railway communication, the writer has taken every opportunity in his power to agitate the matter, and has watched closely the discussions which have been going on in reference to Government Aid towards assisting to build a Railway through the Free Grant Districts. Fortunately, he was present in the House, when the Act to aid in the construction of Railways was brought forward, and, finding that immediate action was necessary, he hurried home and had a meeting called—Geo. F. Gow, Esq., Reeve, in the chair—at which the subject was discussed.

A deputation, consisting of Jno. Teviotdale, Robt. E. Perry, and Thomas McMurray were appointed to go to Toronto in order to secure the extension of the Toronto, Simcoe and Muskoka Junction Railway to Bracebridge.

On Tuesday afternoon, the 14th inst., they left Bracebridge, and the next morning they reached Toronto just in time to see the House prorogued.

An interview was sought with the Attorney General, and at nine o'clock the following morning the deputation, accompanied by the Hon. Frank Smith, Mr. Fred. Cumberland, M.P.P., Mr. Wm. Lount, M.P.P., Mr. A.P. Cockburn, M.P.P., and Mr. Wallis, M.P.P., met at the office of the Attorney General, and were received most graciously by the Premier.

Having received the assurance, that $4,000 per mile would be granted by the Government between Washago and Bracebridge, the Deputation afterwards met the President of the Board, Mr. Cumberland, Mr. Lount, and Mr. Cockburn, at the "Queen's Hotel," when the following arrangement was entered into, subject to the endorsation of the different Reeves and approval of the ratepayers of the district.

"TORONTO, 16th February, 1871.

"MESSRS. TEVIOTDALE, PERRY,
      AND MCMURRAY, Bracebridge.

"GENTLEMEN.—Adverting to your interview with the Attorney General this morning, when you presented a petition from the Muskoka District, praying that the Government would recognize the Toronto, Simcoe and Muskoka Junction Railway as entitled to Parliamentary aid to Bracebridge, under the Act just passed, I understood the Attorney General to say that the Ministry would so recognize that Railway and would apply the aid to its construction as far as Bracebridge, so soon and whenever the Company was in a position to satisfy the Government of its ability to command the remainder of the capital and to construct the Road within the period (six years) limited by its Act of Incorporation.

"It is clear, therefore, that if we can establish that ability *at once*, we can *at once* get Bracebridge declared as the Northern Terminus of the Line, and we can secure the setting apart of a grant in aid of say $4,000 per mile for every mile actually constructed within the Free Grant District.

"We have, as you are aware, surveyed the line of location throughout to Bracebridge, and we have before us the estimates of the cost of the line to that point.

"We have made very beneficial arrangements by lease with the Northern Railway Company, under which a very important portion of the necessary capital is secured; but at present we are unable to do more than secure the means for completing and uniting the line as far as the Portage in the Township of Rama.

"We are nevertheless satisfied that if the Municipalities comprised within the District of Muskoka can contribute by bonus say not less than an aggregate sum of $50,000, being equal to $2,000 per mile, we may be enabled to submit such a scheme for securing the whole capital as will induce and justify the Government in passing an immediate Order of Council securing the aid to Bracebridge as aforesaid.

"In the absence of such assurance from the Municipalities, we see no prospect or ability for projecting our line beyond the Portage, and we shall have (at any rate for the present) to restrict our appeal to the Government for aid in that point.

"I have, therefore, to inquire whether you are prepared to give to my Board of Directors such an assurance of assistance by By-law to the extent of $50,000 as will warrant them in submitting the whole scheme to the Government at once.

"Should you do so, it will be upon the understanding:—

"1st. That the By-law shall await the demand of the Company, and shall only be submitted to the people when the Company is prepared to commence the execution of work.

"2nd. That when and so soon as the By-law shall be passed, the debentures of the county shall be placed in trust, only to be issued from time to time in proportion to the work actually done between Washago and Bracebridge.

"If you assent to these suggestions, it is our conviction that the announcement of the fact, that provision has been secured for the construction of our line to Bracebridge, will give such an impetus to the settlement of your District, as that when (say a year hence) the By-law comes to be submitted, the strength of the township will have been so increased as to make the burthen of the bonus a very light one. The truth is, that your townships are now paying, in extra freight, charges enough to cover all the liability upon a debt double in amount to that which (under the wise provisions of the Government) will now suffice to secure you Railway connection with Lake Ontario and all the markets.

"I am, gentlemen,

"Your obedient servant,

"FRANK SMITH,

"*Pres. of T.S. & M.J. Railway.*"

TORONTO, 16th February, 1871

"THE HON. FRANK SMITH,

    "President, T.S. & M.J. Railway,

        "Toronto.

"SIR,—In reply to your letter of this date, we beg to say that your statement as to the result of our interview with the Attorney-General is correct. Our interpretation of his reply was to the effect that the Government and Legislature did not desire to limit the extension of any railways into Free Grant Districts, but would grant aid under the terms of the Act to such an extent as the Companies could show their ability to construct within the periods named in their charters.

"We quite recognize the importance, therefore, of your being in a position to satisfy the Government of your ability to construct your Railway to Bracebridge, in order that, under the terms of the law, the Government aid may at once be set apart for that purpose.

"We feel satisfied that if it can be at once announced that the Railway to Bracebridge has been recognized by the Government and will be built, our townships will settle up with great rapid-

ity, and will be ready and willing when called upon to contribute
by bonus the amount you require to complete your capital, and
under the securities you suggest.

"We accordingly feel warranted in giving you the assurance
that, when called upon (that is to say, whenever you are ready
actually to commence work), our townships will grant an aggregate bonus of $50,000 in aid of the railway between Washago
and Bracebridge, such aid to be contributed from time to time in
proportion to the work actually executed between those points
—that is to say, at the rate of $2,000 per mile, or say $10,000 for
every section of five miles actually constructed.

"As we are only acting under subordinate powers, it is our
intention at the earliest possible moment to call together the
Reeves of the respective townships, who, we cannot doubt, will
approve and support the action we have not waken, and who will
themselves officially communicate to you the decision at which
they may arrive.

"We are, sir, your obedient servants,

"JOHN TEVIOTDALE,
"ROBT. E. PERRY,
"THOMAS McMURRAY."

MEETING OF THE REEVES OF MUSKOKA.

In accordance with a requisition from the Railway Delega-
tion, the Reeves of Muskoka met at Orange Hall, Bracebridge,
on Wednesday, March 1st, 1871.

On motion of Geo. F. Gow, Esq., Reeve of Macaulay, Mr.
McMurray was appointed Chairman, and Dr. Bridgland Secretary.

The Chairman on rising gave an account of the interviews
which the Deputation had had with the Hon. John S. Macdonald and the Hon. Frank Smith, President of the T., S. and M.J.
Railway, and read the correspondence which had taken place;

after which Messrs. Teviotdale and Perry addressed the meeting. After which all the Reeves expressed themselves in favour of the scheme, and the following letter was forwarded to the President of the T., S. and M.J. Railway:—

"BRACEBRIDGE, 1st March, 1871.
"THE HON. FRANK SMITH,
        "President of the T., S. & M.J. Railway, Toronto.
    "SIR,—At a meeting of the Reeves of the District of Muskoka, at which all were present, it was moved by A.H. Browning, Esq., Reeve of Monck, and seconded by Albert Spring, Esq., Reeve of Draper, and carried unanimously:—

    " 'That this meeting fully endorses the action of the Deputation who have just returned from Toronto, after having had interviews with the Honourable the Attorney-General and the officials of the T., S. and M.J. Railway, and return them its thanks for the trouble they have taken in the matter.

" 'G.F. GOW,
        " 'Reeve of Macaulay.
" 'RODK. STUART,
        " 'Reeve of Muskoka.
" 'A. SUFFERN,
        " 'Reeve of Watt.
" 'DAVID HOGABOAM,
        " 'Reeve of Stephenson.
" 'A. SPRING,
        " 'Reeve of Draper.
" 'A.H. BROWNING,
        " 'Reeve of Monck.' "

———

ANNUAL AND SPECIAL MEETING OF THE TORONTO,
SIMCOE AND MUSKOKA JUNCTION RAILWAY.

On the first day of March, 1871, the above meeting was held in

Toronto, and we have much pleasure in submitting the following from the report of the Hon. Frank Smith:

"6. Your directors have continued to exert great efforts to secure the prosecution of the works to the Muskoka terminus at Bracebridge; and they are encouraged in the belief that, under the application of the recent Railway Subsidy Act, and with the co-operation of the Municipalities of the District, there is no practical obstacle to the accomplishment of that object early in 1873."

COMPLIMENTARY BREAKFAST.
(From the *Northern Advocate* of February 17th, 1871).

"On Tuesday last, it having been ascertained that A.G.P. Dodge, Esq., of the extensive lumbering firm of Dodge & Co., would visit Bracebridge on his way to the Magannetawan, a number of the principal merchants of the place waited upon that gentleman on his arrival and invited him to a complimentary breakfast at the "Dominion House." A large number sat down, the chair being occupied by G.F. Gow, Esq., Reeve of Macaulay, and the vice-chair, by R.E. Perry, Esq. After a liberal discussion of the good things provided, Mr. Dodge was presented with the following address:—

" 'RESPECTED SIR,—It is with feelings of unmingled pleasure that we greet you on the present occasion, in order that we may have the happy privilege of extending to you a sincere welcome to Bracebridge, the centre of your business operations in the District. Nothing affords us greater pleasure than to encourage enterprise and promote the development of this important and rapidly growing section of country and, satisfied that Dodge and enterprise are synonymous terms, and that your operations in this place are calculated to promote this great object and promote the public weal, we hail with delight your visit. Without any flattery we may be allowed to add, that, in addition to the very extensive nature of your operations, the highly honorable manner in which it is conducted has made your name a household word in every home throughout the District, and induced us to take this opportunity of testifying our esteem.

" 'The high position which you occupy, as vice-president of the Toronto, Simcoe & Muskoka Junction Railway, is another inducement which prompts us to the performance of this duty. Convinced as we are that the construction of this line would materially benefit this country, and conscious of the deep interest which you have taken in the promotion of this scheme, we rejoice to have this opportunity to return you, in the name of the settlers, our hearty thanks, with the request that you will use your influence to hasten the day when we will be blessed with Railway facilities. Your first address at the meeting of officials of the Northern Railway, which was held at Parry Sound on the 6th of September last, wherein you remarked, 'I am no annexationist; I believe in individuality; I want to see a spirit of emulation between the two great nations, and to be for ever united in those two great bonds—Friendship and Commerce, together with the friendly spirit which you have manifested towards our Queen and country, the noble philanthropic utterances which you have made when alluding to our Institutions, and the great liberality which has shown out in your every act, have endeared you to our people.

' " We remain, yours respectfully,

"GEO. F. GOW, Reeve.
"JOHN TEVIOTDALE.
"ROBERT E. PERRY.
"THOMAS MYERS.
"J.W. DILL.
"H. PORTAS.
"RICHARD DANIELS.
"REV. JOHN WEBSTER.
"REV. J.R. GIBSON.
"JOSEPH COOPER.

"S. Bridgland, M.D.
"J.N. Byers, M.D.
"E.W. Malpas.
"H.J. McDonald.
"George Wray.
"William Hanna.
"Thomas McMurray.'"
&c. &c. &c.

" 'Mr. Dodge, in reply, said, that he hardly knew how to express his thanks for the kind reception he had met with. He took a deep interest in the progress of the Free Grant Districts, and was desirous to aid in the construction of the Toronto, Simcoe and Muskoka Junction Railway. He expressed himself highly pleased with the kindness which had been shown him since he came to Canada. At Ottawa and in the backwoods he had experienced much friendship, and was now beginning to feel at home with the Canadian people. He had a high appreciation of the merits of the mother country. He recognized that whatever was great, good and grand sprung therefrom; and he anticipated that the great Anglo-Saxon race was destined to make rapid strides upon the continent. He had not as yet allied himself to any of the political parties in this country. He was carefully observing things, and was resolved to identify himself with that party which was best calculated to promote the interests of the people. His highest ambition was to serve the settlers, and he was anxious that all his commerce would prove a mutual benefit.' "

THE

FREE GRANT LANDS

OF

PARRY SOUND.

PARRY SOUND.

About the year 1858, Messrs. J. and W. Gibson erected a saw
mill on the Seguin River, where the Village of Parry Sound now
stands. They continued to manufacture lumber until the year
1863, when they sold out their interest in said mills unto Messrs.
J. and W. Beatty & Co., the present owners. When this change
in the proprietorship took place very little interest was taken
in this section, it being generally considered unfit for settlement, and unfit for agricultural purposes; besides it was almost
completely isolated, as there was no road, and the only way of
reaching it was by sail boat. Up till this time no land had been
surveyed; nor had any ventured to locate there. However, when
Messrs. J. and W. Beatty & Co. took possession, they built a
fine steamer called the "Waubuno," which made weekly trips to
and from Collingwood, thus mail communication was established and means of ingress and egress furnished. On the rec-
ommendation of Messrs. J. and W. Beatty & Co. a road was
opened up between Bracebridge and Parry Sound, a distance of
55 miles; this, together with the enterprize manifested by the
Beattys, gave a stimulus to the settlement of the country. It has
often been asserted that lumberers are opposed to the settlement of the country, but in this case it was not so; instead of
their discouraging settlement, they did everything in their
power to promote it, and the result is patent to all, as the district
is being rapidly filled by a noble class of settlers before whose

presence the forest is being rapidly cleared. It is gratifying to add that since the district has been explored, it has proved more desirable than was at first anticipated, and it is now filling up with great rapidity.

The Government of Ontario offers as a Free Grant to any actual settler over 18 years of age, one hundred acres of land in this District.

Heads of families get two hundred acres as a Free Grant.

Locatees, in addition to obtaining a Free Grant of 100 acres, will be allowed to purchase an additional 100 acres, at 50 cents an acre, cash.

After years of experience and close observation, I give it as my honest conviction that a man of limited means, with a large family of healthy children, cannot do better than by taking advantage of the Free Grant Lands so generously provided, and settling down in the bush; for while they have to work hard, they are free from numerous temptations.

> "Here hardy youths soon learn the axe to wield,
> And drive the steers athwart the frosted field;
> Or pile the firewood on the burdened sleigh,
> Which bears its needful weight the homeward way.
> Here beauteous maidens, household work within
> The homely hut, soon learn to knit and spin—
> To beat the churn, or weave the garment warm,
> While sons and fathers face the bickering storm.
> Here mothers nurse the darling babe, and give
> A helping hand, that all within may live
> In peaceful comfort, and delighted see
> The charms of independence yet to be,—
> When the fair farm is cleared, and debts discharged,
> And the home comforts more and more enlarged."

SITUATION.

The District of Parry Sound is situated on the east shore of the Georgian Bay, and is easily reached in summer by the

Northern Railway from Toronto to Collingwood, thence via steamer "Waubuno" to Parry Sound Village, which is the business centre of the District. It is situated between 80° and 81° west of Greenwich, and between 45° and 46° of north latitude.

BOUNDARIES.

The District is bounded on the south by the Territorial District of Muskoka; on the north by French River and Lake Nipissing; on the east by the District of Nipissing; and on the west by the Georgian Bay.

EXTENT.

The District embraces about forty townships, covering an area of 2,500 square miles; containing about 1,600,000 acres of land, capable of furnishing agricultural homes for at least 100,000 souls.

CLIMATE.

Some persons imagine that the District must be extremely cold, but it is not uncomfortably so. The forest affords much protection, and, situated as it is close to a large body of water, the atmosphere is of a nice even temperature; nor will it ever be otherwise, for there are ridges of rock running through the country which will prevent it from being entirely cleared, so that the District will not be subject to those sweeping currents of air which are so frequent in some of the front townships, and are so trying upon the constitution of man. The climate is exceedingly healthy, and, unless in cases of accident, the services of the doctor are seldom required.

Ague is unknown here, and the District is acknowledged to be one of the most healthy in the world.

Persons who are consumptive will derive much benefit, and, if not too far gone, will be perfectly cured by a short residence in the place,—numbers in the settlement can cheerfully bear testimony to this fact. Here you have complete summer and perfect winter, and enjoy an atmosphere both pure and bracing, which is conducive to the most perfect health.

AS STATED IN THE IMMIGRATION PAMPHLET.

"No where on earth do the seasons of the year move on in lovelier, grander procession. In spring, we have a quick awakening of vegetable life, and nature puts on her best attire, promptly as a bride on her wedding-morn. Our summer is short, but generous with splendour, and bedecked with flowers that can hardly be surpassed; we have oppressive heat at times, and occasionally drought, but how do our summer showers refresh the face of all things; how welcome is the rain, and how green and beautiful are the fields, the gardens, and the woods, when it falls. In autumn we have the waving fields of grain and tasselled corn; our orchards display apples of gold in baskets of silvery verdure, and we can reckon even the grape among our fruits; our forests present a richly-tinted and many-coloured foliage: we have mid-October days in which the weather is superb; our Indian summer is a splendid valedictory to the season of growth and harvest; a bright and beautiful hectic flush sits upon the face of universal nature as death draws on and we glide imperceptibly into winter. This, though confessedly severe, is exhilarating, hardening animal as well as vegetable fibre, while it has its ameliorations and joys in the fire-side warmth that tempers into geniality the clear, frosty air; we have also the merry jingle and fleet gliding of the sleigh, and the skater's healthful sport, together with almost entire exemption from damp and mud, two most disagreeable accompaniments of winter in milder climes. The characteristics of this country are only beginning to be known abroad, as its resources are only beginning to be developed at home. It offers inducements rarely surpassed to industrious, energetic, prudent settlers. Let it only be thickly settled with a population worthy of it, and it will take no mean rank among the countries of the earth. Sunnier climes there may be, but a fitter habitation for the development of a manly, vigorous race, it would be difficult to find in any part of the world."

THE SOIL.

There are some large flats of clay, but the soil is chiefly of a loamy nature, easily worked and admirably adapted to the climate.

As to the precise quantity fit for cultivation in this District, it is impossible to say, but having personally examined the land and being in a position to give a tolerably accurate opinion on the subject, the writer considers that he is under rather than over the mark, when he states that there is at least 70 per cent of land fit for agricultural purposes, in the District, besides, it must be remembered that even the rocky parts will make excellent pasture, and for stock raising is very valuable.

There is a tract of excellent land called the "Oak flats," around Manatawaba lake, 12 miles north of Parry Sound village, which is worthy of attention. Already several settlers have located themselves there, the land is of very superior quality, and the scenery cannot be surpassed in beauty.

The land generally, is rolling, and there is very little swamp.

Stock farming would pay here as cattle thrive well and grass seed and clover grow luxuriantly, even where there is little depth of soil.

WHAT KIND OF TIMBER?

This question is often asked by those who want land, and so much importance is attached to it, that many persons judge of the nature of the soil by the timber that grows thereon. There is great variety however in this respect, the ridges of rock are chiefly covered with pine, and some with oak; the valleys of good land between the ridges are principally covered with hardwood. Maple abounds; elm, basswood, beech and ironwood are plentiful, with some balsam, hemlock and scattered pine.

There is considerable white oak around Manatawaba Lake in the Township of McKellar.

SCENERY.

The scenery is the most picturesque imaginable, the lakes are dotted with innumerable islands, and for beauty and variety cannot be excelled in the Province.

CROPS.

During the past year the crops have been most productive; the settlers have been cheered as well as amply rewarded for their laborious toil.

WHEAT,

The staple of Canada, has been raised here with success; but it must be remarked that in a new country where the clearances are small, this article does not get a fair trial.

OATS

Are a good crop both as regards quality and quantity. On account of the extensive lumbering operations that are carried on, oats are in great demand at high prices. The writer has seen a ten-acre field of as good oats raised here as he ever met with in the "old country."

PEAS

Return a very large yield, and prove a profitable crop to the farmer.

INDIAN CORN

Has been cultivated to advantage, although it is not so sure a crop. The Indians have grown it for years, and we have seen some fields perfectly matured; the success, however, is greatly owing to the season.

BARLEY AND FALL RYE

Have been tried to profit; the latter has been very remunerative, and is a favorite crop with the settlers.

ROOT CROPS.

These grow to perfection in this District. It is admitted that potatoes do best on new soil, and it is astonishing the large yield of roots that may be obtained when properly seen after.

On account of the elevation, and close proximity to the Lake, there is consequently more moisture here in summer than in some older townships, the beneficial effects of which are realized by the settlers, for often they enjoy the most delightful growing weather when farmers outside are suffering from drought.

FRUIT,

So far as it has been tried, has proved successful. Currants and gooseberries grow to perfection; strawberries, of the choicest quality, have been raised, and grapes bid fair for profitable cultivation.

ROADS.

Two leading Colonization Roads branch out from the Village of Parry Sound:—"The North Shore Road," going in a northerly direction towards Sault Ste. Marie; twenty-five miles of this road are already completed, and it will be built as far as the Magannetewan river during the present year. "The Parry Sound Road" takes an easterly course through the Muskoka District.

Another road called "the Nipissing Road," branches off this one at Rosseau Junction, twenty-two miles east of Parry Sound village, and runs in a northerly direction towards Lake Nipissing. At a point on this road, some twenty-five miles north of the Junction, a cross road is being constructed, running west through the townships of Spence and McKellar, until it intersects the "North Shore Road," near Armstrong's Rapids, sixteen miles north of the Village of Parry Sound, where a Post office has been established.

PARRY SOUND.

This village is beautifully situated on an inlet of the Georgian Bay, and can boast of one of the best harbours to be found on the North Shore. Messrs. J. and W. Beatty & Co., the spirited proprietors, have exhibited great taste in laying out the streets, and ornamenting the same with shade trees. From the top of Belvidere you command a delightful view of the bay, dotted with numerous islands; and we may truly say that "Parry Sound, as a summer retreat, can rarely be beat," for the beauty of its scenery, the healthfulness of its climate, and the sport which it affords, will make it always attractive to the admirers of nature. A year ago the District of Parry Sound was formed into a territorial district, for the more ready and convenient administration of justice, and for the registration of deeds and instruments relating to lands of the Province. Consequently a court house is being erected, with registry office and jail, and Mr. J.W. Rose has been appointed stipendiary magistrate. There is a large wholesale and retail store kept by Messrs. J. and W. Beatty & Co. A magnificent saw-mill and grist-mill, owned by the same company; a temperance hotel, boarding house, bakery, butcher's-shop, tinware and stove depot, and drug store, blacksmith shop, post and money order office, school, public library, Wesleyan Church, with resident Wesleyan minister, Church of England minister, and Presbyterian missionary.

At Parry Sound the religious interests of the inhabitants have been well looked after by the spirited proprietors of the place, Messrs. J. and W. Beatty & Co. Here the Wesleyans have a neat church, and preaching twice every Sabbath, together with a prosperous Sabbath School, with Mr. Wm. Beatty, M.P.P., for the superintendent. The Episcopal Church and the Canada Presbyterians have each a missionary stationed at this point.

The following is from the Wesleyan Methodist Missionary Report:—

"In presenting the first Annual Report of the Parry Sound Mission, we desire to record our gratitude to Almighty God, first, for the opening of so wide a door for the triumphs of the Gospel; and, secondly, for the power He has given His Church to enter and present with success the great truths of salvation.

"Five years ago Parry Sound was known only as the hunting ground of the Indians; it is now a thriving village in the very heart of the 'Free Grant Districts.' Immediately after the selection of this place by the Messrs. J. & W. Beatty (worthy Wesleyans), for the location of their large lumbering establishments, a tide of immigration at once set in, and for the accommodation of their workmen, and the incoming settlers, as also for the establishing of our beloved Methodism, Mr. Wm. Beatty, the resident partner, erected forthwith, at his own expense, a neat and commodious Wesleyan Methodist Church, deeded it to the conference, free and unincumbered, and for four years, with the assistance of one or two other brethren, he has conducted public religious service twice every Sabbath, led a class meeting at the close of the morning service, and superintended a flourishing Sabbath school in the afternoon, and regularly sustained also a week-night prayer-meeting; thus from the first, all the means of grace peculiar to our Church have been established and conducted with vigor and success. At the last Conference, however, the work having grown to such dimensions, it was found impossible any longer to carry it on efficiently without the appointment of an ordained minister; accordingly application was made to the Missionary Committee, and the request was granted; and in the 'Minutes' of 1869,

Parry Sound appears for the first time as a regular Conference appointment. During the year, five outside appointments have been established, besides occasional preaching through the settlement. Wherever practicable, societies have been formed, and the entire work placed on a connexional basis. At one of these preaching places a log Church, respectable and neat, has already been built, and arrangements have been made for the speedy erection of two more in other parts of the circuit. With characterized promptness, the Quarterly Board have also undertaken to provide a large and comfortable parsonage for their minister. The building has been commenced, and with the blessing of God upon the work, will ready for occupancy by about the middle of August.

"C.A. HANSON."

The residents of the District are noted for their intelligence and high moral character, and represent most of the religious denominations and different nationalities.

MANUFACTURING FACILITIES.

Water privileges are numerous both in the Village of Parry Sound and throughout the District. There is a splendid opening in the village for a foundry. Stoves, ploughs, and farm implements are in great demand, and the raw material can be laid down here as cheap as in the city of Toronto. Wood, suitable for furniture, is plentiful, and a factory would be remunerative.

NEW TERRITORIAL DISTRICT.

At the last session of the Provincial Parliament, an Act was passed to provide for the organization of the Territorial District of Parry Sound, and for the more ready and convenient administration of justice, for the registration of deeds and instruments relating to lands in that part of this Province, which will be a great convenience to the settlers. This Act furnishes many of the advantages of an independent provisional county, giving both judicial and registration facilities within the District.

Persons arriving in the District now have many advantages over the first settlers. Everything that is required by those settling down on bush farms can be obtained on the most reasonable terms at the village of Parry Sound. Hence parties unacquainted with the requirements of the country will do well to reserve their funds until they fix upon a location, and learn what articles are absolutely wanted, before making their purchases.

WHO WILL SUCCEED?

Men who have been accustomed to labor. Say, those persons who have lived on rented farms in the old country and who possess sufficient means to carry them through until they are able to raise crops capable of supporting their families—such men are certain to succeed. A strong hardy class of men possessing courage and perseverance, with constitutions capable of endurance, assisted by a little means, are sure to get along well in this country, and in a few years to become independent.

The man who comes to take up wild land, having no means to start with, has a poor chance. A married man cannot expect to succeed unless he possess at least two hundred dollars at the commencement.

Of course such persons may hire out and get employment at the lumber shanties or on the Roads, but, while doing so their farms will be neglected.

Some persons have entered the settlement without means and have succeeded well, but at the first they experienced many hardships.

ADVICE TO NEW COMERS.

The new settler on his arrival in the District, should make a thorough examination of the land before locating himself.

There is abundance to select from, and if you do not get a good lot it is your own fault. See that you make a wise choice. Remember it is for life, and your success, or otherwise, to a great extent depends upon the wisdom of this initiatory step.

FISHING.

The Angler can satiate his passion for this innocent sport by following his amusement at some of the numerous Lakes and Rivers throughout this District, which are now noted for the exuberance of speckled trout and other specimens of the finny tribe with which they abound.

TOWNSHIP OF MCKELLAR.

The Township of McKellar abounds with the purest limestone, and is pronounced one of the best that has yet been surveyed in this whole northern section. I have conversed with parties who have explored the entire country from Parry Sound to Lake Nipissing, and they all confirm what I have before asserted, that there is about seventy per cent. of good land in the District. It is important that new townships be at once surveyed, and thrown open to settlers. Already numbers have squatted down upon the unsurveyed lands in Hagerman and elsewhere. One very pleasing feature in connection with this District is the superior manner in which the roads have been made. The bridges are very substantial, and are protected by side railings; while the crossways and bridges are two feet wider than in most places. This, I am told, is entirely due to Mr. Wm. Beatty, M.P.P., who had the roads built in this improved way. I cannot conclude without stating that I was much impressed with the character of the inhabitants of Parry Sound and surrounding country. They are orderly, industrious and intelligent; they are respectable in their appearance, tasteful in their dress; their houses are clean, and their gardens would be a credit to any city in the Province. Flowers and vegetables flourish here most luxuriantly, in producing these articles, while both the climate, the soil, and the situation seem most favourable to their culture. I partook of some of the largest and best gooseberries I have seen since I left Auld Scotia.

The *Globe* of the 22nd September, 1869, contains the following:

"It may not be out of place to draw these notes to a conclusion with a word or two about the inhabitants of Muskoka and Parry Sound, and the land they live in. The most striking characteristic of these people is the remarkable spirit of contentment which generally prevails among them, and the readiness and vigor with which they repudiate any insinuations against their District. We came into contact with hundreds of them, and there was not one of them that did not stand up for Muskoka as energetically as an Irishman or an Englishman would maintain the glory of ould Ireland or merry England."

A REMINISCENCE.
Deputation of Officials of the Northern Railway of Canada to Muskoka and Parry Sound.

In response to the invitation given, a short time since, by the Reeve of Muskoka to the Managing Director of the above road, a large and influential deputation of the officials of the N.R. Co., with other prominent men, arrived on the evening of the 6th Sept., 1869, by the steamer "Wenonah," at Bracebridge the business centre of the Muskoka District. Although the weather was unfavourable, the attendance was large and respectable. The Reeves and leading men turned out well, and evinced a deep interest in railway extension.

The party consisted of the Hon. J.B. Robinson, President; F. Cumberland, M.P.P., Managing Director; Mayor S.B. Harmon; Alderman Baxter; Alderman Dickey; D. Crawford, Esq.; C.W. Moberly, Chief Engineer; Hon. Col. Grey, M.P., New Brunswick; A.P. Dodge, Esq., New York; R.J. Reckie, Esq., Montreal;

Capt. May, Bell Ewart; the Toronto press was also ably represented.

On the 7th a public dinner was given to the deputation at Gravenhurst, at which A.J. Alport, Esq., J.P., Reeve of Muskoka, presided. It was got up in excellent style, and reflected great credit upon the spirited proprietor, Mr. B. Fuller. A public meeting was also held, when able and interesting speeches were delivered by the President, Managing Director, Col. Grey and others. The remarks made indicated a willingness on the part of the Company to deal liberally with the people of these new districts, and if the settlers will only do their part, the Northern Railway Company will meet them as far as possible in these matters.

On the 8th the party left the Village of Gravenhurst by steamer "Wenonah," and proceeded to the Indian Village at Port Carling. After a sail on Joseph River, they partook of luncheon on one of the beautiful islands, after which they started in the steamer "Wabamik" to Nipissing Junction at the head of Lake Rosseau, where they arrived safe and sound after many adventures by the way, and found a home for the night at Mr. Irwin's Hotel, where the host and hostess gave them every attention. Here they were met by Mr. William Beatty, M.P.P. A very pleasant night was spent, and it is due to Alderman Baxter to state that he contributed greatly to the hilarity of the occasion.

On the morning of the 9th the party left in four conveyances, which had been provided by Mr. Beatty, and proceeded to Parry Sound. The weather was all that could be desired. The sun shone brightly—adorned the face of nature, and at 4 o'clock in the afternoon they arrived, and were greeted with a hearty welcome by the inhabitants, who took quite an interest in the reception. The Village looked quite gay, with flags flying at the custom house, post office, mill, hotel and other places, while the steamers and sailing vessels in port vied with each other as to which would make the grandest show. The steam pleasure yacht "Mittie Grew," owned by A.J.P. Dodge, Esq., was tastefully decorated with flags and streamers representing the different nations. The stars and stripes waving in the breeze side by side with the glorious old union jack. The "Wave," owned by Messrs. J. and W. Beatty & Co., was also in gala attire, having been furnished with a complete set of new flags for the occasion.

After luncheon at the Seguin House, the party were shown the principal places of interest in the village, among which were the Mills, printing establishment of the *Northern Advocate*, Belvidere and the Camp Ground. Teams were then in readiness, and the party had a pleasant drive up the North Shore Road, where they had a delightful view of Mill Lake, and the Cascades on the Seguin River. On their return, dinner was announced, to which the party with others sat down, and partook of one of the best dinners that could be provided in Ontario. The bill of fare was sumptuous, and the table elegantly decked with beautiful flowers. Great praise is due to Mr. and Mrs. Blair, of the Seguin House, for the manner in which dinner was served up, both as regards the variety brought forward and the style in which everything was prepared. Mr. Wm. Beatty, M.P.P., filled the chair with his usual ability, and all went merry as a marriage bell. After ample justice had been done to the good things so liberally provided, a beautiful supply of pure cold water was freely furnished, and the Chairman rose and said, "gentlemen, fill your glasses;" he then gave the first toast, "The Queen and all the members of the Royal Family," which was drank with all honors. Song—"God save the Queen," led by Alderman Baxter.

"The Governor and Lieut. Governors of the Dominion," came next, and was drank with enthusiasm.

The third toast was "The Army and Navy," to which Aldermen Baxter and Dickey, replied.

A good deal of merriment was caused by the skirmishing of

those two gentlemen, and for once we fear, the former got slightly wounded.

"The Dominion Parliament," was responded to by Col. Grey, M.P., of New Brunswick, in a very able and racy speech, he said he came to examine the country and to make the acquaintance of the Canadian people, and being a member of the Dominion Parliament, he considered it nothing more than his duty to do so. He expressed that he had been most agreeably surprised; that the country was much better than he expected, and he considered it capable of great fertility; as regards the roads, he thought that the less he said about them the better.

The Colonel anticipates great things for Parry Sound, and expects that it will become a town of importance before ten years.

"The Local Legislature," was replied to in a very neat and eloquent address by the efficient Managing Director of the Northern Railway, F. Cumberland, Esq., M.P.P.

"The Mayor and Corporation of the City of Toronto," was the next given, and heartily responded to by S.B. Harman, Mayor, who, in replying, stated that the scenery through which he passed was most romantic, the lakes and rivers extremely beautiful, and that pleasantry and good humour had characterized the trip.

He spoke strongly in favor of Railway extensions, and his address was graceful and practical. The mayor has made many friends by this trip. We congratulate the City of Toronto on having so popular a representative.

"Success to the Northern Railway." The Hon. Jno. B. Robinson replied in a practical speech, noted for the strong, good common sense views which he expressed, and the information which he conveyed.

"North Shore Development." A.G.P. Dodge, Esq., replied to this toast in a speech which gave evidence of high moral training, advanced mental culture and deep research. His allusions to the "Pilgrim Fathers" was most touching. His statements that the North Shore of the Georgian Bay is rich in iron ore and other minerals, is valuable, and the development of this North Territory is only a matter of time. Although Mr. Dodge is an American, and the son of the distinguished American Philanthropist, the Hon. W.E. Dodge, of New York, yet he is no annexationist, hear him, "I am no annexationist, I believe in individuality, I want to see a spirit of emulation between the two great nations, and to be ever united in those two great bonds, Friendship and Commerce."

P.S. Gibson, Esq., P.L.S., of Willowdale being present, was called upon by the chairman to make a few remarks, and we consider that his address was one of the ablest that was delivered during the evening, his remarks were practical and pointed. In alluding to the roads he said that we were not to be looked upon as beggars when we asked for a grant of money to build and repair roads; that we only asked back a part of what the Government had already received for the timber which they had sold. He also advocated the opening up of cross roads in addition to main leading roads.

"The Press,"—This toast was replied to by Mr. Cunningham, of the *Globe* who will give his views upon the country in letters which will appear in that paper to which we intend to refer on some future occasion. The Editor of the *Northern Advocate* also replied, giving a short history of the Muskoka District, and in the name of the people, gave the guests to understand that should they see fit to return again we would give them a hearty welcome, and try to keep the friendship that had been formed, as pure as the clear water in which it had been drank.

The last toast, "Success to the firm of Messrs. J. and W. Beatty & Co.," was proposed by the Mayor of Toronto. Mr. W. Beatty, M.P.P., rose, and, in a very feeling and eloquent address, thanked the gentlemen present for the hearty way in which the toast had been responded to. He said that some of the happiest years of his life had been spent in the Sound; that he loved to mark the progress that was going on in a new settlement; that much of the praise that had been ascribed to him was due to the Northern Railway Company; that only for it he would not have invested here.

After "Auld Lang Syne" and "God Save the Queen" were sung, the company broke up, at the wee hour beyond the twelve. In referring to the bad state of the roads, several of the speakers expressed their deep regret that the Hon. S. Richards, Commissioner of Crown Lands, was not with them.

On the morning of the 10th, the party went out in the steamers "Mittie Grew" and "Wave" for a delightful sail among the islands of the bay. The sky was clear, and the reflection most perfect, and all enjoyed the trip amazingly. The steamer "Waubuno" having arrived, the party went off to Byng Inlet. As the steamer left the wharf, three hearty cheers were given to the deputation as they moved out of sight.

THE ROUTE.

Parties wishing to settle on the Free Grants in the Parry Sound territory, may proceed by either of the following routes:—

1st. From Toronto to Barrie or Bell Ewart by the Northern Railway; from thence to the River Severn by steamer; from the River Severn to Gravenhurst, on Lake Muskoka, by stage; from Gravenhurst to Bracebridge by steamer, or by the Muskoka Road; and from Bracebridge to the respective townships by the Muskoka, Peterson and Parry Sound Roads. In winter the communication with Bracebridge and Parry Sound is by stage from Barrie. A company is now formed to construct a railway to connect with the Northern, from Barrie to Muskoka District. The office of C.W. Lount, Esq., Crown Lands Agent for the

Townships of Watt, Stephenson, Brunel, Macaulay, McLean, Muskoka and Draper, is at Bracebridge in the Township of Macaulay.

2nd. To Collingwood from Toronto by the Northern Railway; from Collingwood to Parry Sound by steamer, once a week, every Saturday morning, during the summer months; and from Parry Sound to the respective townships by the Great Northern, Parry Sound, and Nipissing Colonization Roads. A stage runs from Parry Sound to Lake Rosseau, connecting with the steamer. The office of John D. Beatty, Esq., Crown Lands Agent for the Townships of McDougall, Foley, Humphrey and Cardwell, is at Parry Sound.

BYNG INLET,

The seat of the extensive lumbering operations of Messrs. Dodge & Co., and Messrs. Clarke, White & Co., is situated on the Maganetawa River. A very large amount of capital has been expended here, and considerable improvements have been made of a very substantial nature.

The following extracts from the Surveyor's Reports will give the reader a good idea of the district.

MCDOUGALL

Is situated in the county of Simcoe. It is bounded on the north by unsurveyed territory, on the east by unsurveyed territory, on the south by the township of Foley, and on the west by the Georgian Bay.

This township contains an area of about 70,000 acres of which 43,864 acres (water and roads included) were subdivided in 1866, by Provincial Land Surveyor, J.L.P. O'Hanly.

The following is an extract from Mr. O'Hanly's report of survey:—

"This township has considerable diversity of surface and soil.

MUSKOKA AND PARRY SOUND 159

The surface is generally flat, having few elevations 100 feet above the level of Georgian Bay. Yet it is much broken both by hills and lakes. The hills for the most part are abrupt and precipitous, falling and rising by steps like a terrace, gradual slopes being rare. The land in many places is of the worst kind, being almost destitute of mould or verdure, while in other parts it is well adapted for settlement.

"On the accompanying trace I—by different colors, in a general way—indicated the land fit for settlement, as well as the bad land. Not that I would be understood to mean that no part of that shewn bad is fit for settlement. I have no doubt but small patches here and there will be found intermixed with it of a very fair quality, and so of the other, as some spots will be found in it very inferior. But for a general and comprehensive classification I think it may be relied on as pretty accurate, indeed as correct as it is possible to do it without a special inspection.

"The timber consists of birch, maple, pine, hemlock, beech, balsam, ironwood, oak, cedar, basswood, spruce, tamarac, ash, elm, poplar and birch. This is the order of predominancy. There is a great deal of white pine, but much scattered and therefore very difficult to fix its limits, except along the valleys of streams and the margins of lakes, and Parry Sound. Along the latter there is much of inferior quality and stunted growth. It is nowhere to be met with in groves, and not often in clumps, yet there is scarcely a spot without it; and the country, viewed at a distance, would be probably considered as a vast pinery. Red pine is entirely unknown.

FOLEY

Is situated in the County of Simcoe. It is bounded on the north by the Township of McDougall, on the east, south and west by unsurveyed land, the north-west corner of the township touching on Parry Sound.

It was surveyed in 1866 by Provincial Land Surveyor George A. Stewart, and contains an area of 42,497 acres, including water and roads.

The following is an extract from Mr. Stewart's report of survey:—

"The Parry Sound Colonization Road passes diagonally through the township from south-east to north-west, thus facilitating in the best possible manner the settlement of the township. This road, through Foley, is of a very superior quality, and will compare most favourably with any of the colonization roads with which I am acquainted, and reflects great credit on the parties employed in its construction.

PHYSICAL FEATURES OF THE COUNTRY.

"A large proportion of this township is occupied by water, a characteristic common to his portion of the Province. The lakes throughout this township are generally very irregular in outline, presenting bold rocky shores and great depth of water. An examination of the map will shew the position and extent of these lakes. It will be observed that towards the western part of the township they become more numerous and irregular as we approach the Georgian Bay. These lakes present scenery of singular beauty and variety, and possess many attractions to the sportsman and tourist.

"The hills throughout the township are generally rugged and rocky, presenting in some cases impassable barriers.

"The rivers are of small dimensions, connecting the several lakes. The principal river, after passing through several lakes, continues its course westerly along the tenth concession, and empties into Parry Sound near the western boundary of the township. It has several falls in its course which might be made available for manufacturing purposes. The position of these falls is indicated on the plan and field notes.

"A lake of some magnitude occupies a considerable portion of the centre of the township. It is named by the Indians Nig-ga-go-bing.

"Land of excellent quality will be found in several places along the southern boundary, particularly from lot number one to number eight, and from fourteen westward to lot twenty-four. Towards the western end of this boundary the land becomes rougher and more broken, although still containing small patches of good land. At the south-west angle of the township a very extensive marsh occurs, which rendered it difficult to continue the survey to that corner.

"This township is principally watered by the River Seguin, which enters it from the east by two branches, the northern at lot No. 1, in the 8th concession, flows southerly a distance of about five miles; and the southern branch at lot No. 1, in the 4th concession, flows westerly a distance of three and a half miles; uniting at lot No. 11, in the 5th concession, flows westerly a distance of three miles, makes an acute angle with its last course, flowing south-easterly enters Mill Lake at two miles, then forming the outlet of Mill Lake flows south-westerly one and a half miles into Parry Sound.

"At its mouth is situated the nucleus of the town of Parry Sound, and lumbering establishment of Messrs. J. & W. Beatty & Co. There is a church, a post and customs offices, a hotel, and two stores and several mechanics. There are about 20 houses, principally occupied by the employees of Messrs. Beatty & Co.

"Between the village and foot of Mill Lake there are three separate rapids, to obviate which there is a very fair portage road. At the foot of Mill Lake there is a fine water privilege, and an excellent site for a mill, on which the Messrs. Beatty have erected a dam and made other improvements to facilitate the descent of saw-logs and husband the spring's flood for the summer's consumption, of which Mill Lake is the reservoir. This chute is about 18 feet high.

"Mill Lake, the largest inland lake in the township, is very pic-

turesque with its deep bays, bold bluffs and pretty islands. From
Mill Lake to the forks there is very little obstruction to the navigation, except in the dry season that it becomes very shallow
and unsafe for bark canoes.

"From the forks, for about two miles, the north branch is
composed of a series of rapids and cataracts, alternating with
small basins of still water. The navigation here is wholly imprac-
ticable. The scenery is extremely wild and romantic. There are
many water privileges which are not likely to be useful within a
reasonable time, and therefore, for the present at least, absolutely worthless. To obviate this there is a canoe route by
Trout Lake, and two smaller ones, and entering the north
branch at the head of these rapids. From this to the eastern
boundary, the river may be called three narrow, shallow lakes
divided by three short rapids, where it crosses at the foot of the
chutes from Manatawaba Lake.

"The south branch, from the forks to the eastern boundary,
has but one small rapid, but nearly the whole way it is swift and
shallow. This stream, as far as I have seen it, is well adapted for
the descent of saw-logs and timber.

"There are primarily two conditions essential to the success
of a new settlement. The first is good land, and the second cheap
and expeditious access to markets or centres of trade; without
both these conditions new settlements cannot flourish, and it is
unfortunate they seldom go hand in hand. The former to raise
abundant crops, and the latter to dispose of them at remunerative prices. I have seen new settlements, where the land was of
good quality, in a very languishing condition for want of the
other. For without competition the redundant crop is sold at a
sacrifice, whilst purchasable necessaries are exorbitantly high.

"Though this township has not the first condition in a pre-
eminent degree, yet it has a good deal of land well calculated to
recompense industrious labour, and has very superior advantages in the second condition, as a steamer weekly plies between

Parry Sound and Collingwood, and thence by rail to Toronto; so that Parry Sound, in the summer season, is in direct communication with all the civilized world. Besides the route is both cheap and expeditious, leaving Parry Sound in the morning and reaching Toronto in the evening; about 180 miles for $4.85 cents.

"Such facilities of communications are of vast advantage to the settler, and cannot fail to give a great impetus to the speedy and successful settlement of this section of the new country, a progress, without which, it would not make in another quarter of a century."

HUMPHREY

Is bounded on the north by unsurveyed land, on the east by the Township of Cardwell, on the south by Lakes Rosseau and Joseph and unsurveyed land, and on the west by unsurveyed land.

This township was sub-divided during 1866 and 1867 by Provincial Land Surveyor Gibbs, and contains an area of 49,596 acres, including water and roads.

The following is an extract from Mr. Gibbs' Report of Survey:—

"The Township of Humphrey embraces an area of 49,596 acres, about 12,496 acres lying under the waters of Lakes Rosseau, Joseph and sundry others of less size. The two first-named extend across a considerable portion of the south part of the township, and are, in great part, environed by hilly banks, with here and there high and precipitous rocks of gneiss, syenite and others of granitic and quartzose character, which kinds prevail pretty generally throughout the adjacent country.

"The surface, although a good deal broken in this manner, is finely diversified, with rolling hills and land more slightly undulating, covered with a growth of heavy timber, consisting of maple, beech, birch, bass ironwood, hemlock, white pine and other kinds common to this section of country; also tamarac, balsam, spruce, cedar, black ash, and alder swamps; beaver meadows, with an exuberant growth of grass (the "blue joint"), cranberry marshes, and some portions too rocky for cultivation; the whole interspersed with lakes and small streams, in the greater number of which flows clear and limpid water.

"The streams, being inconsiderable in size, do not afford many permanent privileges for machinery; but the falls situated on both sides of the north boundary of concession B, upon Oak Creek, which is the largest stream in the township, I have no doubt will be found a great convenience for mill purposes to the settlers. Skiffs and canoes have access for upwards of about two miles from the mouth of the creek, at low water; and it could be made available for driving pine logs and timber, several miles from Lake Rosseau, in the spring of the year.

"The lakes and streams abound with fish, in variety, as salmon and speckled trout, white-fish, pickerel, bass, perch, suckers, &c.; and there is ample scope for the sportsman along their banks and in the adjacent woods in pursuit of game; deer, rabbits and partridge are especially plentiful. In the forest the bear, the wolf and the fox are frequently met; and furred animals, such as the beaver, mink and muskrat, although long sought after by the Indian trapper, are yet to be found.

"A portion of the tract of high land situate between the north-westerly bays of Lake Rosseau and Lake Joseph, together with a strip of land extending along the easterly boundary line northward from the Parry Sound road, and along the north boundary next the north-east angle of the township, comprising about 8,000 acres, being much broken with rock, affords little inducement for settlement; but, after making this deduction, I believe the township generally contains more good land than most others recently surveyed, with which I am acquainted. The rich loamy soil of the higher land, not rocky, is well suited for agriculture, and will doubtless produce excellent crops of the different kinds of roots and cereals adapted to the climate, and the low lands produce most luxuriant grass—a great advantage to the early settler in feeding and raising stock.

"During the past season, peas, oats, Indian corn, potatoes, turnips, tobacco, melons and sundry productions, were cultivated by the few settlers present, with much success.

"Since I left the township I have been informed that several respectable families have moved in; and I believe that, with the increased facilities of access, by the opening of the Parry Sound road and the Nipissing road line, together with the Muskoka Lake steam navigation, through the enterprise of A.P. Cockburn, of Gravenhurst, during the past season, it will be speedily settled."

EXPLORATION LINE BETWEEN SPANISH RIVER AND PARRY SOUND.

The following is an extract from Provincial Land Surveyor Fitzgerald's report of survey of exploration line for a road between Spanish River on the north shore of Lake Huron, and Parry Sound on the east shore of Georgian Bay, in the year 1865:—

"From the Maganatewan, south to Parry Sound, are several hardwood tracts of land, though a portion of the country has a partially broken surface. On the whole, I consider this tract capable of affording a fully 60 to 75 per cent. of arable land. It is covered in places with exceedingly fine beech and maple, while other parts yield a fair growth of pine, hemlock, &c., and if opened up for settlement, and proper facilities held forth, would in a short time become a thriving locality.

"At Parry Sound the nucleus of a promising village has already been established. A magnificent saw-mill, owned by the Messrs. Beatty, is now in constant operation, and affords employment to a number of men.

"Though perhaps not more than one-half to two-thirds of this territory is actually fit for settlement, yet, in view of the immense quantity of valuable pine timber, of the undoubted mineral wealth yet undiscovered in this region, of the many important fishing stations along the north shore, of the construction of a canal via the French River, and above all, being our only land connection with the Great North-West Territory, the subject of annexing which to Canada at present occupies so large a share of the public mind. Yet I say, in view of these considerations, the country will doubtless, ere long, become a scene of active and energetic occupations, and form the home of many a happy and prosperous settler."

ONTARIO.

Ontario is the largest and wealthiest Province of the Dominion of Canada. It comprises forty-three fine large counties, and four new judicial districts, viz: the Algoma, Nipissing, Muskoka and Parry Sound. There is but one Legislative Chamber in this Province, the House of Assembly, composed of eighty two members, elected by the people for four years. Population of the Province, nearly 2,000,000; of the capital, the City of Toronto, about 60,000.

LIEUT.-GOVERNOR: HON. W.P. HOWLAND, C.B.

EXECUTIVE COUNCIL: HON. J.S. MACDONALD, Premier and Attorney General.

HON. S. RICHARDS, Commissioner of Crown Lands.

HON. JOHN CARLING, Commissioner of Public Works and Agriculture.

HON. M.C. CAMERON, Provincial Secretary and Registrar.

HON. E.B. WOOD, Provincial Treasurer.

PUBLIC OFFICERS
FOR MUSKOKA DISTRICT.

STIPENDIARY MAGISTRATE—C.W. Lount, barrister, Bracebridge.

REGISTRAR—C.W. Lount, barrister, Bracebridge.

CROWN LANDS AGENT—C.W. Lount, barrister, Bracebridge.

DISTRICT SEAT—Village of Bracebridge.

PUBLIC OFFICERS
FOR PARRY SOUND DISTRICT.

STIPENDIARY MAGISTRATE—J.W. Rose, Parry Sound.

REGISTRAR—J.W. Rose, Parry Sound.

CROWN LANDS AGENT—John D. Beatty, Parry Sound.

DOMINION OF CANADA.

EMIGRATION

TO THE

PROVINCE OF ONTARIO.

To Capitalists, Tenant Farmers, Agricultural Labourers, Mechanics, Day
Labourers, and all parties desirous of Improving their
Circumstances by Emigrating to a New Country.

The attention of intending Emigrants is invited to the great advantages presented
by the Province of Ontario. Persons living on the Interest of their Money can easily
get EIGHT PER CENT. on first-class security.

TENANT FARMERS WITH LIMITED CAPITAL,

Can buy and stock a Freehold Estate with the money needed to carry on a small farm
in Britain. Good Cleared land, with a Dwelling and good Barn and out-houses upon
it, can be purchased in desirable localities, at from £4 to £10 sterling per acre.

Farm hands can readily obtain work at GOOD WAGES.

Among the inducements offered to intending Emigrants, by Government, is

A FREE GRANT OF LAND!

WITHOUT ANY CHARGE WHATEVER.

Every Head of a Family can obtain, on condition of settlement, a Free Grant of
TWO HUNDRED ACRES of Land for himself, and ONE HUNDRED ACRES
additional for each member of his family, male or female, over eighteen years of age.

All persons over Eighteen years of age can obtain a Free Grant of ONE HUN-
DRED ACRES.

The Free Grants are protected by a Homestead Exemption Act, and are not liable
to seizure for any debt incurred before the issue of the patent, or for twenty years
after its issue. They are within easy access of the front settlements, and are supplied
with regular postal communication.

REGISTERS OF THE LABOUR MARKET

And of Improved Farms for sale, are kept at the Immigration Agencies in the Province,
and arrangements are made for directing emigrants to those points where employment
can be most readily obtained. Several new lines of Railway and other Public Works
are in course of construction, or about being commenced, which will afford employment
to an almost unlimited number of labourers.

Persons desiring fuller information respecting the Province of Ontario

Are invited to apply personally, or by letter, to the Canadian Government Emigration
Agents in Europe, viz: WM. DIXON, 11 Adam Street, Adelphi, London, W. C.;
J. G. MOYLAN, Dublin; CHARLES FOY, Belfast; DAVID SHAW, Glasgow;
and E. SIMAYS, Continental Agent at Antwerp.

Also to the Immigration Agents in Canada, viz:—JOHN A. DONALDSON,
Toronto; R. H. RAE, Hamilton; WM. J. WILLS, Ottawa; JAS. MACPHERSON,
Kingston; L. STAFFORD, Quebec; J. J. DALEY, Montreal; E. CLAY, Halifax,
Nova Scotia; ROBT. SHIVES, St. John, and J. G. G. LAYTON, Miramichi, New
Brunswick,—from whom pamphlets, issued under the authority of the Government of
Ontario, containing full particulars in relation to character and resources of, and the
cost of living, wages, &c., in the Province, can be obtained.

JOHN CARLING,

*Commissioner of Agriculture and Public Work
for the Province of Ontario*

DEPARTMENT OF IMMIGRATION
Toronto, March, 1871.

NORTHERN RAILWAY
OF CANADA.

IN CONNECTION WITH THE
FREE GRANT DISTRICTS
OF
PARRY SOUND AND MUSKOKA.

Land given away to all comers over 18 years of age. A family of several persons can secure a large block of land gratis.

The Government of Ontario offers as a Free Grant to any actual settler over 18 years of age, One Hundred Acres of Land in the Free Grant Districts.

Heads of Families get Two Hundred Acres as a Free Grant.

Locatees, in addition to obtaining the Free Grant of 100 acres, will be allowed to purchase an additional 100 acres at 50 cents an acre, cash.

TRAINS MOVING NORTH

Leave the Company's Stations, City Hall and foot of Brock Street, Toronto, as follows :—

	A.M.	P.M.
City Hall	7.00	4.00
Brock Street	7.15	4.15

Fare from Toronto to Bracebridge, - - - - **$3.75.**

CONNECTIONS.

BELL EWART—With Steamer *Emily May*, leaving Bell Ewart every morning, on arrival of Mail Train from Toronto, for Beaverton, Orillia and intermediate ports on Lake Simcoe, connecting with steamer for Washago : also stage for Gravenhurst, and steamer *Wenonah* for Bracebridge and ports on Lake Muskoka, and steamer *Wabamik* for ports on Lake Rosseau. With steamer *Simcoe*, leaving Bell Ewart every evening on arrival of Express Train from Toronto, for Orillia direct, returning to Bell Ewart connect with Morning Express Train for Toronto and Collingwood.

BARRIE—Daily stage to Penetanguishine. With steamer *Ida Burton*, leaving Barrie at 5.30 a.m. daily for Orillia and Washago, connecting with stage for Gravenhurst, and steamer *Wenonah* for Bracebridge and ports on Lake Muskoka, and steamer *Wabamik* for ports on Lake Rosseau.

COLLINGWOOD—The steamer *Waubuno* leaves Collingwood every Saturday morning for Parry Sound.

FRED. CUMBERLAND,
Managing Director.

ABOUT THE MAP

THOMAS MCMURRAY'S 1871 edition of *The Free Grant Lands of Canada* contained in the back a 15- by 19-inch fold-out Ontario government map, titled *Map of Part of the Province of Ontario, Canada*, "compiled and prepared for the Department of Public Works from the latest govt. surveys, maps, &c. &c. by W.J.S. Holwell, P.L.S., 1871."

At a scale of 20 miles to the inch, and encompassing all of southern Ontario south of Lake Nipissing, the map depicts counties and townships, towns and settlements, railways and colonization roads, and the lands then being offered for free grant settlement. The free grant lands, mainly on the southern edge of the Canadian Shield, included those described by McMurray in Muskoka and Parry Sound, as well as townships farther east, in Haliburton, Peterborough, Hastings, Frontenac, and Renfrew counties.

In this edition of McMurray's book, on the facing page, we have reproduced a portion of the map—that part showing the free grant districts of Muskoka and Parry Sound, and the access to them from the south. The townships offered at the time for free grant settlement are shaded.

Muskoka and Parry Sound districts are not named on the map, although they did exist as official geographic entities by 1871. Not until 1888, however, were the townships and municipalities in the two districts actually separated from the counties to the south.

A copy of the entire map may be viewed on the Fox Meadow web site (www.foxmeadowbooks.com/1871map.html).

River Railway, and now the certainty of the construction of the Toronto, Simcoe & Muskoka Junction Railway to the village of Bracebridge is a fixed fact. While, at the same time, it possesses a very large extent of country, 70 per cent. of which is fit for cultivation, and its water facilities are unsurpassed on the American continent. The importance of the water-power which this country contains cannot be over-estimated. It is designed to be an important manufacturing country, and may one day be the very workshop of Canada itself. As a stock-raising country it will stand unrivalled in the Province ; besides, minerals have been found in sufficient quantities to satisfy even the most incredulous, that this whole section abounds with the richest treasures which will be developed at no very distant date. As for stock farming, Muskoka will be to Ontario what the Highlands of Scotland is to the Lowlands of Scotland. It will be a great nursery for sheep and cattle ; the land is both high and roll-ing ; it is well watered, and a very rich grazing country, and when it becomes linked by the Railway to Toronto the market will be very little inferior to that great centre. Then there is considerable timber, both pine and hemlock, and, as it is now demonstrated that the latter contains an extract which is very valuable, it must prove an increasing source of wealth. Competent judges say that it is worth 20 per cent. more than pine timber.

It is now generally admitted that Muskoka possesses many advantages, and that it has made rapid progress.

THE FIRST NEWSPAPER.

The first newspaper in the Settlement was published by the author, on the 14th day of September, 1869, bearing the title of the " *Northern Advocate.*" It was first printed at Parry Sound, but from the fact that Bracebridge was more central it has been removed thither. The object of the publisher was to give reliable information about the Free Grant Lands, and his labours have been very successful. The circulation is 1,000 copies weekly. A great many copies go to England, Ireland and Scotland for the information of intending emigrants, and through its advocacy many have been induced to settle in our midst.

It is somewhat singular, that when the writer first came to Muskoka, he had to row across Muskoka lake, and when the first issue of the *Northern Advocate* was published, it so happened that the steamer was under repairs, and he had to row 16 miles across the same water in order to deliver the first number.

PRODUCTION NOTES

1871 EDITION

———

At left is a reproduction, at actual size and with approximately the same margins, of a page from the original edition of *The Free Grant Lands of Canada*. The book was printed by the letterpress process (metal type) at the *Northern Advocate* office in Bracebridge, then shipped to Toronto for binding. It featured sewn signatures with a hard cover; the book opened flat, allowing the narrow inside margin. The light-weight, acidic paper has become thin and brittle with age.

The first edition had 160 regular pages (xii + 146 + 2 full-page advertisements at the end). It also included the fold-out map, inserted after page 146, and two wood engravings on a pink-coloured stock—one a portrait of McMurray inserted preceding the title page, the other a view of South Falls inserted preceding page 31. Trim size was 5 ⅝ by 8 ¾ inches. The cloth over the cover boards had a maroon, enamel-like coating with a textured surface, into which decorative patterns were stamped to give the appearance of tooled leather. The short title, *Muskoka and Parry Sound*, was gold-foil-stamped on the front cover and spine (McMurray's name appeared on the front too).

NOTES

PAGE 1: "The Road was commenced ..." This was the Muskoka Colonization Road. It was open to South Falls (Muskoka Falls) in 1860, North Falls (Bracebridge) in 1861, and Huntsville in 1870.

PAGE 5: "The Soils." Many surveyors and others in the 19th century mistook the hardwood forests of Muskoka and other parts of the southern Canadian Shield as an indication of rich soil—after all, similar forests had cloaked the lands farther south. Although the thin, sandy Shield soil produced amazing yields for a few years after the land was cleared, it was quickly depleted by intensive cropping in all but some isolated pockets of richer bottomlands.

PAGE 17: The railway did come soon to Muskoka, but not as far as McMurray and others hoped. It reached Severn Bridge in 1874 and terminated on Lake Muskoka at Gravenhurst in 1875 (by then it was part of the Northern Railway). With access to the Muskoka Lakes navigation and the timber resources of the Muskoka River, the railway company was in no hurry to extend it farther north. Not until 1886, after considerable debate about the route, was the line opened through Bracebridge, Huntsville, and beyond to North Bay, an extension primarily made to connect with the Canadian Pacific.

PAGE 19: "Two miles up the Severn River are the falls; ..." The reference is to Wasdell's Falls.

PAGE 21: "Muskoka Falls." The height is often exaggerated in early accounts, McMurray's figure of 175 feet being no exception. The total natural drop was about 100 feet at the main chutes (South Falls) at the Muskoka Road bridge, and another 30 feet at the Hanna Chutes a short distance upstream.

PAGE 34-35: McMurray homesteaded by Trethewey's Falls ("Draper Falls"). This land was better suited for farming than that in many parts of Muskoka. The Trethewey family settled here in the 1860s, and remained after McMurray departed.

Originally, the first Muskoka settlers had to travel to a grist mill near Orillia to have their grain ground into flour. There was a post office at Severn Bridge in 1861, and Muskoka Falls in 1862. By 1864 Bracebridge had both saw and grist mills, as well as a post office.

PAGE 55: Hemlock bark is rich in tannin, once used in leather tanning, and Muskoka soon became an important centre for the tanning industry. The first tannery opened in 1877 at Bracebridge, and two more large ones were established in the early 1890s, one each in Bracebridge and Huntsville.

PAGE 81: "Beaver River" in Muskoka Township. This was the Hoc Roc River; the principal tributary of this stream is still called Beaver Creek.

PAGE 81: "Watt township is in the county of Simcoe." In the early years the townships and villages in Muskoka and southern Parry Sound districts were attached to adjacent counties to the south, Simcoe and Victoria, for municipal purposes.

PAGE 95: "Experimental townships." In the 1870s, the so-called "Donaldson Colonization Scheme" was tried in Ryerson Township, in Parry Sound District west of Burk's Falls. (This was not one of the townships McMurray was responsible for as Crown Lands Agent in Parry Sound.) On selected lots, the government had five acres cleared and a house built; settlers paid $200 for the property and could gain title by staying at least five years and clearing 10 more acres. However, the $200 wasn't always collected up front, as intended, and the plan proved financially unsustainable because some settlers could not or would not make their payments. By the late 1870s 58 families had been settled under the scheme.

PAGE 160-61: Foley Township—"The principal river, after passing through several lakes ..." This is the Boyne River. "Lake Nig-ga-go-bing" is Otter Lake.

The part of the description of Foley Township beginning with the paragraph "This township is principally watered by the River Seguin," actually belongs to the preceding description of McDougall Township.

PAGE 164: "Oak Creek." This was White Oak Creek, soon to gain renown for its beauty under the more poetic name Shadow River. In the 1860s, after the surveyor passed through, Ebenezer Sirett built a water-powered sawmill at the "mill privilege" mentioned.

PAGE 166: "... a canal via the French River." A plan, often proposed but never implemented, to provide navigation from the St. Lawrence River at Montreal to Georgian Bay by a canal utilizing the Ottawa, Mattawa, and French rivers.